ROUTLEDGE LIBRARY EDITIONS:
HIGHER EDUCATION

Volume 16

THE STUDENT EXPERIENCE OF HIGHER EDUCATION

THE STUDENT EXPERIENCE OF HIGHER EDUCATION

IAN LEWIS

LONDON AND NEW YORK

First published in 1984 by Croom Helm Ltd
This edition first published in 2019
by Routledge
2 Park Square, Milton Park, Abingdon, Oxon OX14 4RN
and by Routledge
52 Vanderbilt Avenue, New York, NY 10017

Routledge is an imprint of the Taylor & Francis Group, an informa business

© 1984 Ian Lewis

All rights reserved. No part of this book may be reprinted or reproduced or utilised in any form or by any electronic, mechanical, or other means, now known or hereafter invented, including photocopying and recording, or in any information storage or retrieval system, without permission in writing from the publishers.

Trademark notice: Product or corporate names may be trademarks or registered trademarks, and are used only for identification and explanation without intent to infringe.

British Library Cataloguing in Publication Data
A catalogue record for this book is available from the British Library

ISBN: 978-1-138-32388-9 (Set)
ISBN: 978-0-429-43625-3 (Set) (ebk)
ISBN: 978-1-138-33026-9 (Volume 16) (hbk)
ISBN: 978-1-138-33035-1 (Volume 16) (pbk)
ISBN: 978-0-429-44795-2 (Volume 16) (ebk)

Publisher's Note
The publisher has gone to great lengths to ensure the quality of this reprint but points out that some imperfections in the original copies may be apparent.

Disclaimer
The publisher has made every effort to trace copyright holders and would welcome correspondence from those they have been unable to trace.

THE STUDENT EXPERIENCE OF HIGHER EDUCATION

IAN LEWIS

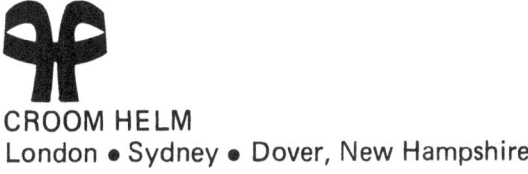

CROOM HELM
London • Sydney • Dover, New Hampshire

© 1984 Ian Lewis
Croom Helm Ltd, Provident House, Burrell Row,
Beckenham, Kent BR3 1AT

Croom Helm Australia Pty Ltd, First Floor, 139 King St.,
Sydney, NSW 2001, Australia

British Library Cataloguing in Publication Data

Lewis, Ian
 The student experience of higher education.
 1. College students–Great Britain–
 Case studies
 I. Title
 378'.198'07222   LA637.7

ISBN 0-7099-1666-3

Croom Helm, 51 Washington Street, Dover,
New Hampshire 03820, USA

Library of Congress Catalog Card Number: 84-45557
Cataloging in Publication Data applied for.

Printed and bound in Great Britain
by Billing & Sons Limited, Worcester.

CONTENTS

List of Tables

Acknowledgements

1.	INTRODUCTION	1
	Justification	1
	Structure	14
	Context	18
2.	BECOMING A STUDENT	29
3.	IMPLICATIONS OF STUDENTS' USE OF LIBRARIES	50
4.	BEING A MATURE STUDENT	68
5.	BEING AN OVERSEAS STUDENT	90
6.	BEING A WOMAN PHYSICS STUDENT	109
7.	THE STUDENT EXPERIENCE	128
8.	THE CONSEQUENCES FOR HIGHER EDUCATION	148
	Immediate Consequences	149
	Effective Student Learning	153
	Research in Higher Education	161
	Future Developments in Higher Education	166
References		172

TABLES

1.1	Gender Balance (percentages)	23
1.2	Age Range of York Entrants	24
1.3	Choice of York	24
1.4	Regional Distribution of Entrants	24
1.5	Entrants' Previous Institution	24
4.1	Age Profile of Responding Mature Students	74
4.2	Subject Balance of Respondents	74
7.1	Mature Students' Perceptions of Differences from other Undergraduates	137

ACKNOWLEDGEMENTS

Without the commitment and thoroughness of four student researchers this book could not have been written, and our knowledge of significant aspects of the student experience would be substantially reduced. Victoria Billington, Barbara Gillie, Ursula Newell and Elizabeth Rothschild, through being students whilst conducting their research activities, were able to add two critical dimensions to this work: (a) they were able to mix easily with other students and so provide a significant element of ecological validity to their findings; (b) they were able to offer critical insights and interpretations which others, being removed from the student world, might easily have missed.

To make the most of the relationships between their separate studies, the author has written the relevant chapters of this book from their own reports. This has been done to ensure consistency of presentation, and to allow the cumulative effects of the separate studies to be brought to the fore. To preserve the immediacy of the originals, though, the first person has been used, and it is hoped that readers are not confused by this. The University Registrar gave permission for the use of university documents which helped to provide the detailed picture of the University which is offered in Chapter 1, and which also provided a basis for comparison in Chapter 4. It is, however, the author's picture of the University which is presented and not, in any sense, an 'official' view.

Philip Hills, the series editor, provided substantial support from the original conception through the various stages of publication, and made many helpful suggestions to improve the substance and structure of the book. Hazel Haines did wonders

Acknowledgements

in producing the final typescript of the manuscript. Martin Scargill drew the site plan in Chapter 1. Many colleagues, and particularly Frankie Todd, played a part in shaping different parts of this book, either through comments at seminars where original versions were first presented, or else through comments on drafts of various chapters.

The author is grateful to all the above individuals, and also to the many hundreds of students who provided, wittingly or unwittingly, the raw material of their perceptions of and reactions to different aspects of their university experience.

Ian Lewis
University of York

Chapter 1

INTRODUCTION

We know very little about the world of university students. In spite of the substantial expansion of universities since the publication of the Robbins Report (1963) and in spite of current preoccupations and attendant publicity about the future of universities, few people in this country have ever had direct experience of the student world. Figures in Social Trends (1982), for example, indicate that less than 30% of the adult population possess graduate qualifications and, given the various routes by which these may be acquired, such a figure over-represents the extent of first-hand experiences of the world of the university student.
This book represents a small attempt to rectify that situation by offering, in five of its eight chapters, accounts of different aspects of the student experience in one small campus university - York, in the north of England. We shall attempt to offer, in this introductory chapter, some of the reasons why the book has come to be written, some preliminary justifications for the approach adopted by the studies to be reported, an indication of the later arguments to be developed out of the findings to be presented. The chapter will continue with outline descriptions of the different aspects of the student experience which will be presented and will conclude with a brief description of some features of the university in which the research was undertaken.

Justification
It has been a salutory experience to find, in preparing the book for publication, that there does not exist, in this country, a comparable collection of published studies based on the same university to which they could be related. This novel feature - of

Introduction

a series of studies of student views conducted in
the same university - will also be explored in the
book in later chapters, but preliminary comment will
be made in this introduction about the predominant
tradition of research into student performance in
British universities. The absence of a British
equivalent to an already influential and long-
standing American tradition will form a necessary
part of this context-setting introduction. Where
possible, though, attempts will be made to link this
collection of studies with the small number of published reports of single studies in a variety of
other universities. The common features of many of
these will allow the later possibility of generalisation from one highly specific university context
to be made with some justification.

All this is not to say that little has been
written at all about British students. We can find
out, from a variety of statistical sources (UCCA,
DES and UGC, are three main sources in their annual
reports), about the courses students take, the
relative popularity of universities, the range of
student entry qualifications, the eventual degree
performances and occupational destinations as students leave their universities and enter society.

Formal research studies, on varying scales,
have also attempted to analyse and correlate a
range of student attributes - such as degree class
and later career development - with such other factors as social class, parental education and personality characteristics. Some of these studies have
also tried to delve into the examination of different student approaches to learning. Perhaps the
most notable and wide ranging of these in Britain
in recent years have been, respectively, the work
of Halsey, Heath and Ridge (1980) and Entwistle and
Wilson (1977). The latter has also formed part of
a continuing series of related studies and a good
bibliography is to be found in Wilson (1982).

However, how students feel about being students,
what is important to them, what affects their progress, are things not readily discovered in spite of
a proliferation of such research.

Universities are, at present, the subject of
much continuing public and political debate about
whether society is getting value for its substantial
investment in higher education. The question of
loans or grants as the main means of financing students, given initial impetus by Maynard (1975), and
more recently aired by the present Minister of State
for Education, is but one of the issues in the

Introduction

present debate. The UGC has also become involved through having to implement the government's proposals for an overall reduction in both student numbers and university expenditure. The National Advisory Board - the recently constituted equivalent to the UGC and concerned predominantly with the public sector institutions of higher education - is also in the process of examining ways of reducing the costs and increasing the cost-effectiveness of those institutions with which it is statutorily concerned.

Other influential groups, like the Group for Research and Innovation in Higher Education, funded by the Nuffield Foundation, in the 1970s, produced a variety of reports which examined a range of alternatives to traditional lecture courses, and made many insightful suggestions about course designs felt to be more suitable to changing circumstances in higher education. Similarly, and more recently, the reports of the seminars organised by the Leverhulme Programme of Study into the Future of Higher Education, for example, Wagner (ed), (1982), indicate widespread, influential and international concern with appropriate administrative structures more suited to projected future developments both within society and in higher education.

Psacharopoulos and Layard (1979) underpin much of the public concern with a highly technical analysis of data involved with developing an economic model to explore the relationship between levels of educational qualification and life-time earnings. In this paper they gave a particular technical slant to a series of questions about the future of higher education initiated by the D.E.S. (1978) in its very influential - if since substantially superseded - Discussion Document examining a range of alternative possibilities.

This rather cursory survey of a range of recent and influential approaches to a variety of questions affecting the nature and extent of higher education in general and university education in particular serves to demonstrate one major point. This is that in spite of much high level intellectual concern - and the above references can only outline the extent and variety of this concern - with analysis of higher education, our present state of understanding of the university world is similar to the state of knowledge of the world of school so effectively criticised by Young (1971). In his introduction to that seminal collection, he noted that in spite of the proliferation of extensive enquiries into the

Introduction

effects of schooling throughout the post-war years, "by treating as unproblematic 'what it is to be educated', such enquiries do little more than provide what is often a somewhat questionable legitimacy to the various pressures for administrative and curricular 'reform'," (p.2).

Although new directions were followed subsequent to the publication of Young's book, it took further developments in the Open University to give substantial impetus to our general understanding of 'what it is to be educated'. Hammersley and Woods (1976) were amongst the first to provide a significant opportunity for insight into the child's world of school by incorporating a number of original reports on pupil cultures into their course reader. As they note in their introduction to this interesting collection: "Pupils' constructions are largely new territory, though there have been many representations of them through secondary filters. Too often they have been represented or studied in official terms and within official categories as 'succeeding' or 'failing', 'choosing options' ..." (p. 6).

This book - and the individual studies it contains - is based on two premises: that since any decisions about universities will affect students, it is as well to know something about their experiences; and that since a deeper understanding of the world of schools has emerged once a concern for process and direct experiences became a feature of research, it is high time that similar developments took place in the world of research into universities.

The various studies to be reported upon - outline details will be given later in this chapter - were each conducted in an attempt to understand more fully the nature of a particular aspect of the student experience at university. In each case the work was done because it was felt by the researcher that there were significant issues to be explored within the area of concern. These issues arose either from reflection on personal experience, or else were the result of an interest stimulated by some external change. In each case there was an initial suspicion that many university students were not benefitting as fully as they might from the opportunities which a university place, in principle, made available.

If any institution is examined solely in terms of cost-effectiveness it is necessary to discount from consideration many aspects of the complex

Introduction

realities of the experiences of those directly involved. This would be as true in an industrial as in an educational context. Similarly, to treat the student experience solely, or largely, in terms of examining correlations between their entry qualifications, personality characteristics, socio-economic background factors and eventual degree performance, occupational entry and life-time careers can conceivably lead to significant misrepresentation within the analyses. Such approaches can also lead - as they clearly did for many years in studies of school performance - to a lack of concern with factors which are crucial to the students' own perceptions of their experience.

The stimulus for the work to be reported on here came from three sources: (a) a growing recognition that university students were becoming increasingly interested in questioning aspects of their university experiences. Throughout the late 1970s, as public debate began to concentrate on exploring alternative futures for higher education, N.U.S. debates frequently covered questions about the nature of effective higher education in addition to their more publicised discussions and statements about large-scale political issues. Such questioning was also a feature of more parochial debates on individual campuses. (b) a small-scale study, funded by the Nuffield Foundation's small-grants scheme, of the student reaction to the introduction of a modular course structure in the undergraduate education course at the University of York. Since this has been reported elsewhere - see Lewis and Vulliamy, 1978 and 1981 - it will not be included in this volume, but a number of the findings which emerged raised disturbing questions about the possibility of a substantial gulf between faculty and student perceptions. The search for other similarly focused interpretive studies of the student experience indicated that, apart from a few isolated instances, there had (and still has) been little work done in this country other than within the large-scale quantitative tradition to describe the student experience. (c) The final influence arose directly out of consideration of this last point. Given that there appeared to be a significant lack of interpretive studies based within a single British university, that, in itself, could be taken as sufficient justification for an attempt to redress a serious imbalance. However, given that academic sociologists appeared to be quite happy to look at any other educational institutions than their own,

Introduction

and that the emergence of an interpretive ethnographic tradition in the sociology of schooling had produced such interesting and far-reaching results, this was also seen as a further justification for developing such an approach within one's own university. The final stage in this line of development followed once it was found that there were sufficient students with both research experience and similar interests who wished to embark on studies of aspects of the student experience which interested them.

It is salutory to be reminded of the fact that whilst a substantial amount of research has been done into aspects of university life and experience, there is still nothing in this country to match the work of Becker and Merton in America. Neither in relation to ethnographic studies of particular faculty experience, as reported in Merton et al (1957) and Becker et al (1961), nor in respect of a detailed study of life on one specific campus, as recounted in Becker et al (1968), do we have comparable British examples. In consequence, except in terms of individual small-scale instances, it is not really possible to determine the extent to which one of the main conclusions from the last Becker study exist in this country. Yet, in terms of that conclusion, it must be of great importance to know whether or not a similar situation exists in our universities since the implications, were this to be so, are very wide-ranging indeed.

Becker and his team concluded their analysis as follows:

> But the faculty view is faulty. It assumes that student performance depends solely on ability and interest and ignores the complicated network of social relations, group definitions, and obligations in which students find themselves ... It underestimates students' rationality in attempting to meet and satisfy the many demands made on them. It fails, in short, to give full weight to the socially structured conditions of student performance. (pp. 130 - 131)

If such a situation is characteristic of the official view within British universities then there must be a serious problem attached to any consideration of new patterns of courses, any changes in patterns of entry or degree requirements, or any discussion of new patterns of administrative needs

Introduction

which fails to take into account the nature of the experiences as perceived by the students - who will, after all, form the bulk of those members of a university who might be affected by any changes.
 A similar problem must be attendant on any consideration of psychological theories of learning and their implications for course design if such theories do not - because of the significant lack of relevant evidence - take into account the varying realities of student experiences in the process of learning. To rely predominantly, as such theories must because of the nature of the kinds of evidence which are available, on information derived from personality inventories and questionnaire completion, or to extrapolate from developmental theories which presume that the adult state is the end-point of learning complexity, must be to misconceive the nature of the actual experiences of learning which the students themselves undergo. Such positions must, by the very nature of the limited and restricted evidence on which they draw, be at best only a very partial reflection of a complex social world. At worst they could reflect a major misrepresentation of the student experience and, in consequence, provide a basis for changes which might not be in the best interests of enhanced learning and optimum benefits for future generations of students.
 One further element of justification for this book rests on the fact that all the studies to be reported took place within the same university. The institutional context is thus held constant and each study benefits, eventually, from the cumulative potential of its neighbours. It is important to stress, though, that we cannot and do not claim to have in any sense replicated the unified approach of Becker and his colleagues in their detailed study of life at the State University of Kansas. We do, however, claim to be able to offer the first opportunity in this country to examine a range of aspects of the student experience on one particular campus university based on evidence emerging from a series of descriptive/interpretive enquiries. The concentration, therefore, is on the issues which emerged once we began to chart the experiences of students as they saw them, rather than upon any attempt to evaluate pre-determined hypotheses drawn from the literature.
 An additional justification, then, lies in the fact that while we do not parallel American work, our researches have sufficient similarity in two

Introduction

major respects - restriction to one campus, and adherence to an interpretive research strategy - that the possibility of making connections with the earlier American work exists. We have already noted the significant conclusion which emerges from one of these American studies. In spite of the fact that it is nearly twenty years since even the last of those studies was undertaken, and in spite of the fact that American and British universities are organised on somewhat different principles, the importance of the American results is such that even a remote possibility that something similar could emerge here more than warrants undertaking appropriate enquiry.

It does follow, though, that we will not necessarily be able to generalise our findings to all students at all universities. However, as with any reports based on interpretive studies, it is possible for any reader to make a personal comparison based on their own experiences. Features of our students' experiences may bear striking similarities to those of students in very different university settings. Such generalisations as might emerge will form the basis for the penultimate chapter of this book, in which we shall draw the threads of the different studies together. This, though, can only be done if we can show that in spite of the different focus of attention of each study there appear to be singular features which run through them all. If, in addition, we are in a position to make connections with the American studies, and also show similarities with the other small-scale interpretive studies which are beginning to be published, then the basis for potential generalisation becomes more substantial.

There are certainly indications in a number of these small-scale studies that the real world of university students is exceedingly complex. Shattock and Walker (1976), for example, studied the attitudes influencing student choices of university for the whole of one year's intake at Warwick. They found, amongst other things, that there were many signs of students 'shopping around' for 'best buys' amongst the universities which offered them places. Such 'shopping around' did not consist of aimless or irrational choices. Nor, however, did it consist of simply weighing up the different kinds of courses they were offered in the various institutions. A whole range of factors was involved in any individual decision to take up an offer from Warwick. Many of these factors were to

Introduction

do with matters affecting the student's personal life - family and other relationships. Others were to do with expectation of social life. Still others were concerned with career prospects.

The overall picture which emerged was one which characterised these students as not being solely, nor in many cases centrally, concerned with academic interest in course content, structure and organisation. Academics concerned with university entry know this. A look at any university prospectus will confirm the fact. Such documents contain a large body of information about university courses but they also include a wide variety of other information about life at university and a range of other than academic features of that university's situation. Many of these prospectuses are well and copiously illustrated, and the range of illustrations often reflects a very wide perspective on the student world. (There is, incidentally, a brief but interesting study to be conducted into the presentation of universities through their prospectuses. Some have changed significantly externally and internally; others appear to present an unchanging image.)

In spite of this public recognition that there is more to university life than academic courses and examinations, the main academic pre-occupation with students, once they have arrived at university, revolves around the work relationship. Most staff-student contact is functional and remains fixed within the lecture, seminar or tutorial framework. The rest of the world of the student - the social, political and personal world - tends to be treated as the students' own private domain. University staff only rarely play any direct part in this world. The working relationship between staff and students is predominantly focused on the academic setting within a formal teaching and learning context.

Other, more personal supervisory contacts do, undoubtedly, take place. Staff do expect, and frequently find, that students talk over problems with them. This is important, and rightly considered to be so. Studies of student failure, like Miller's (1970) substantial report, or approaches to student counselling like the recent study by Wright (1982) of work done at Reading, all indicate that personal problems can seriously affect a student's capacity to cope with academic demands. Not surprisingly, Gibbs's (1981) approach to helping students to learn more effectively, devotes sub-

Introduction

stantial attention to developing awareness of the range of demands, in addition to the academic one, with which students have to cope. However, in much of the literature there is very little concern with students who do not appear to have any serious problems, whose work appears to be progressing normally. Such an attitude, though, begs the question of what counts as normal within the student experience. Students are constantly beset with problems. Coping with the demands of their courses presents a paramount source of problems for most students during most of their university life.

Miller and Parlett (1974), in their study of Edinburgh students, showed how a significant concern for the students lay in unravelling what they thought to be the hidden rules of the 'examination game'. The authors state that:

> it is part of the hidden curriculum ... that the student has to decide which pieces of work can be 'selectively neglected' out of the mass of set work; or which particular method of doing problems will get the highest marks. (p. 51)

In other words, even completing a university course satisfactorily is not a straightforward activity. Even if courses are well planned and described in great detail, students appear to discern significant differences in the ways in which different members of staff deal with these courses. Some students actively set out to take advantage of these individual differences, and probed even further to provide great detail on specific tutor biasses. Others were positively alert to anything which could be interpreted as a clue to eventual assessment implications. A third group appeared simply to see these varieties as 'facts' of academic life with no assessment implications of value to themselves, even if they were noticed at all.

Beard (1968), in her now classic study resulting from her work at the University Teaching Methods Unit, London, showed very clearly that many university courses are not always well designed. Quoting particular examples she showed how the actual courses presented, the formal syllabuses and what was eventually measured in assessment did not, in a number of cases match up at all. Even the academic parts of university life are therefore fraught with difficulties for the student trying to cope. Variations in the ways in which courses are mediated

Introduction

by staff compound the intrinsic difficulties which subjects of these courses necessarily contain.
 Mastery of university level courses is not intended to be easy. However, their organisation, presentation and eventual student evaluation all conspire to make them even more difficult. There is at least a need, then, for an understanding of the student reaction to academic work. In this respect a process-product approach is unlikely to provide much in the way of useful insights. Comparison between A-level grades and eventual degree peformance may provide a basis for serious questions about academic entry requirements. Are A-level grades a reliable indicator of performance anyway - a question which emerges from a study of the J.M.B. (1983) report? Perhaps more importantly, in a context when, as a result of UGC implementation of government policy, the proportion of university places available to the appropriate age group is diminishing, there is the question of whether A-levels provide a satisfactory basis for measuring what the Robbins Report (1963) defined as "appropriate attainment and ability to profit from a university course," (para. 31). More important, though, is the fact that by not being concerned to unravel the detail of the intervening undergraduate experience, such studies fail to touch on aspects of that experience which might be even more critical in determining eventual degree performance. It is at least possible that, as with school students, simply coping with the complex world which university students inhabit plays a significant part in determining final levels of qualifications.
 Personality and attitudinal characteristics may also be important. Their value, in terms of helping to understand student performance, let alone in terms of attempting to change student achievement levels, must, however, be questionable. Unless, that is, we attempt to change personalities or take it upon ourselves to modify attitudes in an explicit fashion. Entwistle and Wilson (1977) published the results of the large-scale national sample survey of such relationships between personality and performance. They were able to identify significant differences in students' self-reported work habits. For example, the group who worked very much within the limits they perceived as being laid down by the official syllabuses. Then there was another large group which tended to work more independently, and followed interests of their own as well. At the same time, the authors noted that it

11

Introduction

was only through the additional evidence which emerged from personal and informal contacts whilst conducting their highly structured research, that they gleaned important clues to begin to interpret their findings.

They, too, were forced to recognise the complexity of the social world in which we expect our students to learn. They characterised this complexity through the invention of a board game which they saw as an analogue of undergraduate life. The game consists of plotting a pathway from one end of the board to another, using a number of dice, and with quite complicated rules. It is not the precise nature of the game which matters - although readers might find it interesting, and potential students terrifying, to play - but the very complexity of the experience which is offered. Complexity, too, which emerges as a result of only partial informal contact with the student world.

If the focus of much research into the university world is narrowly conceived it is not, perhaps, surprising that academic staff, with their own professional research interests, also appear, in general, to have narrow interests in aspects of the student experience - other than a functional concern, which has increased in recent years with the relative cuts in intake numbers, with entry qualifications and eventual satisfactory degree performance. That such a state of affairs should still persist twenty years after the publication of the Robbins Report is difficult to explain. However, a brief examination of some of the consequences of the Robbins Report may shed some light on this state of affairs.

The Report clearly influenced opinion in support of the expansion of university provision through the 1960s and 1970s - although the inauguration of a number of the 'new' universities in advance of the publication of Robbins suggests that the ground was already well prepared. In addition, and as part of the argument, the Report drew attention to the famous 'pool of ability' - those adults who were found to have the potential to cope with undergraduate courses but who had left school well before they could have acquired appropriate entry qualifications. At the same time, the Report noted some disturbing features of 'wastage' rates - numbers who failed to complete their university courses. By raising these issues the Robbins Committee provided a suitable basis for the reception of two other reports on aspects of university

Introduction

teaching, the Hale Report (1964) and the Brynmor Jones Report (1965).
These two reports took different approaches to the question of how university teaching could be improved. As McAleese (1979) has pointed out, one was more concerned with approaches through educational technology - course design, assessment methods and teaching aids - whilst the other was more concerned to establish effective methods of training for university teachers. In this latter respect it is worth recalling the comments of Jacques Barzun (1968):

> University teaching is thus the only profession (except the proverbially oldest in the world) for which no training is given or required. (p. 36)

Although we can, perhaps, add that the two professions can readily be distinguished in terms of the extent to which they are demonstrably aware of and react to the needs and expectations of their clients!

What is of interest here about the subsequent history of the above two reports is that the educational technology approach became the dominant concern. There has, therefore, been much rethinking of course structures and design. There is a wide proliferation and use of a variety of technical aids in university teaching. University teachers, though, still do not have training as teachers as a condition of appointment or tenure. Promotion, too, is still predominantly based on research expertise.

Thus the structured features surrounding the professional circumstances of academic staff are likely to reinforce an orientation which limits severely the need for and the capacity to be directly concerned with the whole of the student experience. Startup (1979) has reported an extensive exploration of this academic perspective. While the majority of students complete their courses and get degrees there is no significant source of pressure to examine the contours of the student world. While universities are still in the happy position of having a high demand for undergraduate places, this further diminishes the need for such interests.

The counter-argument, to which this book contributes, has at least two strands. Firstly, that questions of cost-effectiveness and correlational studies between before and after parameters of student performance need also to take into account

Introduction

some real understanding of the whole of the student experience. Why they do what they do, and what factors influence their behaviour are at least as important as any issues connected with the arid world of manpower planning or that of statistical tests of significance. Questions of the relevance of universities to future social and industrial needs are initially bound up with student attitudes, expectations and experiences. Without a full and adequate knowledge of these parameters of future graduates we will not know very much about the full potential which they can offer.

Secondly, it is almost a truism to suggest that the most effective teaching and learning can only take place when teachers are fully aware of the circumstances which influence their students' careers. This has been recognised in respect of school-level education for a very long time. Bernstein (1970) effectively encapsulated the idea in the following assertion:

> If the culture of the teacher is to become part of the consequences of the child, then the culture of the child must first be in the consciousness of the teacher. (p. 120)

It cannot be enough, therefore, to be simply concerned with the 'rude mechanicals' of curriculum design and course relevance. Nor can it be enough to codify and catalogue student replies to personality and attitude test. If student involvement in and commitment to their academic work is important, we need to know as much as possible about things which can influence this. Such understanding can only emerge through attempts to probe and discover "the complicated network of social relations, group definitions, and obligations in which students find themselves." Becker et al, op. cit.)

Structure
The five chapters which follow this introduction provide a basis for the beginnings of a British attempt to match the work developed in America over twenty years ago. While they do not comprise an attempt to provide a total picture of student life at one university, nevertheless they do cover a range of different aspects of student experience within one university. In spite of their diversity of approaches and concerns, they have a

Introduction

number of important things in common:-

(a) they each contrive to present information from the relevant student point of view;
(b) they each operate within a predominantly interpretive rather than quantitative tradition of enquiry;
(c) by holding the academic context in common they are able to relate to each other and complement each other's findings.

In spite of the diversity of concerns which each original piece of research reflected, their similarity of approach allows a cumulative picture to be developed and thus provides a basis for eventual synthesis where findings emerge which cut across the separate enquiries.

We shall begin the presentation of reports based on these studies in Chapter Two, Becoming a Student, which focuses attention on what appears to be the critical period of transition into the student world - the first few weeks of the first year of undergraduate life. This account is based on participant observation study in which the researcher, herself an undergraduate at the time, 'became' a 'fresher' and underwent what turned out to be the confusing and contradictory experience of arriving at the university and being inducted into studenthood. Because of its focus of concern, and because many of the issues it raises are echoed in the subsequent chapters, this is an ideal opening to the book. It highlights, with insight and immediacy, the problems of becoming a student and the substantial gulfs which open between the institutional and personal perspectives which every university must contain.

Chapter Three, Implications of Students' Use of Libraries, presents the results of a detailed and extensive co-operation between a university librarian and the staff of one department of the university. What emerged was two-fold: one element consists of the misleading assumptions which appear to be characteristic of the views and training of university librarians in general, and which leads to their making false assumptions about the way in which students perceive libraries. The other focuses attention on a particular group of History students who are following a course designed

Introduction

to encourage them to develop the skills of professional historians by undertaking small-scale research projects requiring the conduct of original bibliographic searches. What becomes clear is that the way in which students perceive the demands of the course, in relation to assessment requirements and the expertise of their tutor, is very different.

The researcher for Chapter Four, <u>Being a Mature Student</u>, was herself in this particular category and wedded, initially, to the value of experience between school and university. She found, through informal conversation with a range of other mature students that, other than in age, more varied personal experiences and one other factor, mature students were not really differentiable from other students. The other factor which emerged concerned the fact that mature students do, perhaps, have a clearer view of what they expect from their decision to come to university but that, other than in terms of their attempts to ensure that academic staff took their problems seriously, they faced the same problems and difficulties in accommodating to the various and conflicting demands which face all students. Contrast is made with the findings of an official university enquiry into mature students and their problems, conducted by the University Teaching Workshop Committee, and the contrast with the way in which academics appear to interpret mature students' situations is examined.

Another particular sub-group of students forms the basis for Chapter Five, <u>Being an Overseas Student</u>. Given the recent changes in how the government requires that overseas students are defined and charged for courses, this study takes on an importance which was not anticipated. Through a process of informal conversations with a wide variety of overseas students the researcher, herself an indigenous student, discovers a major point of misunderstanding between the official and the personal perspective on the problem of such students. Academics perceive overseas students as having major problems with English and use the evidence of students' lack of socialising to support this view. From the students' vantage point, they appear to be forced into close contact with other overseas students for two main reasons: one because they experience the same problems as any new student, of becoming a member of the university community and, like other students, make initial contacts with others who are similarly placed. The other because they do have language problems, but their problems

Introduction

here are more associated with a lack of colloquial English, which makes communication with indigenous students difficult, than they are with the professional language demands of their academic courses.

Chapter Six, Being a Woman Physics Student, concentrates on some of the findings of a study into how women students perceive the experience of studying in one of the most masculine of all disciplines. Informal interviews were completed with all the women studying Physics at York during one academic year. Interpretation of the results raises questions about two important issues: one of these concerns the interpretations arising out of many school-based studies of girls and science; the other throws a worrying light on these women's views of a university world which is generally seen as unreal, masculine and uninviting. The consequences, in terms of the students' career orientation and the implications of these for any significant changes in the image of Physics and of universities are examined.

Two final chapters use the reports of the separate studies to build up a case for further detailed examination of the student perspective of their university experiences. In Chapter Seven we shall begin the argument by pulling together the significant findings reported in the preceding chapters, to provide a picture of the student perspective. The results allow connections to be made with American studies as well as with the few other British studies operating within the same interpretive tradition. The omissions which appear to result from the predominant British psychometric approach to enquiry into student experience will be further examined. Central to this chapter will be the reinforcement of the view that the university world is substantially different when seen by students and compared with the official perspectives promulgated in prospectuses and course design. The implications of these differences are examined and compared with some recent approaches to similar questions which, in consequence, are seen to be prone to potential misleading developments.

In the final chapter, The Consequences for Higher Education, we shall focus attention on two major questions. The first of these will be the implications for universities - although reference will obviously be made to other sectors of higher education as well - of the research reported earlier in the book. This will be re-examined in the light of changing pressures resulting from reactions to

Introduction

government policies and changing demographic and economic factors. The other will focus attention on the implications of these researches for future policies and practices for research into higher education. Critical to this last part will be the parallels to be drawn with the increasing understanding of the complexity of the educational process at the school level which have emerged from a radically changed research emphasis in the last ten years.

While these last two chapters are likely to be of interest mainly to those involved in research in higher education and in policy making, it is hoped that the bulk of the book will capture the interest of the general reader who is concerned about the educational benefits of university life. By concentrating on the student perspective we hope to show that there is indeed a world of difference between the official and the student views. Through a better understanding of this difference, the possibility of a deeper appreciation of the implications of academic actions at all levels might emerge.

Context

One area of substantial difference, though, for many readers could lie in the nature of the university in which the studies reported here were conducted. We conclude this chapter, therefore, with a brief outline of the University of York and those of its feature which might be seen to have a bearing on some of the more detailed findings which will be offered later. We do this for two reasons: on the one hand to recognise, at the outset, that every institution has its own peculiarities and that these can easily be taken as the norm by those within them. While we shall, in the later stages of this book, explore some generalisations about the university experience which seems to be relevant to all students and all universities we hope to provide, below, sufficient information about our own to allow the reader to judge these generalisations even more critically than might otherwise be the case. Secondly, there is the extension of the reason offered at the beginning of this chapter, that many readers may have at best only a passing knowledge of any aspect of the university world. For this reason, too, there is a need to supply some factual detail about the university within which the students whose experience we recount lived their lives. Unlike Blishen (1983) we see no point in trying to

Introduction

disguise the University of York under a pseudonym. Those in other universities will be in a position to judge the extent to which York differs substantially from their own institution and may also be able to say whether any differences are likely to affect the nature of the kinds of student experience we report.

The details which follow can also provide an alternative to the brief pen-portraits contained in recent articles in the Observer (1983) and Sunday Times (1983) colour magazine articles comparing universities. In these, for example, the University of York was described as "campus, collegiate, arts-orientated ... An insider's comment added: "Hooray Henryish, especially in English and History departments. A mood of apathy and torpor reigns, not helped by the number of Oxbridge rejects."" (Observer, op.cit.). And "the most traditional of the new universities, also considered the most successful: very popular with students, almost untouched by U.G.C. Biassed towards arts and social studies ... emphasis on small-group teaching ... mixture of examination methods ... Union accepts university claim of lower than average drop outs. Easy to change courses. Places for all first and third years in six colleges, all mixed, even on corridors. Staff-student relationships notably informal... A student recommends "warmth and humanity" of place, but warns it is "unadventurously middle-class."" (Sunday Times, op.cit.).

The University of York, the context for the studies used in this book, is one of the 'new universities' developed just before the publication of the Robbins Report. Its present student population is around 3,500 with an annual undergraduate intake approaching 1,000. Like most of these 'new' universities - apart from those which emerged out of technological predecessors in the wake of Robbins - York is also situated in open fields, just outside the boundary of the host city. Whether the nature of these 1960s developments represents some symbolic relationship between the academic and the social world is open to question. These 1960s settings, though, contrast markedly with the late nineteenth and early twentieth century developments of civic universities which were, predominantly, within their major industrial conurbations. The reader interested in making international comparisons on university developments is referred to Driver (1971), and anyone interested in comparisons between the 'new' universities themselves is

Introduction

referred to the series of articles by Wilby (1976).
   The Development Plan (University of York, 1962) produced by the architects indicates that from the beginning there was very close co-operation between them and the Academic Planning Board. It expresses a clearly formulated philosophy to guide both academic and architectural thinking, and this has eventually been made manifest in the physical form and structure of the university. The principles which guided this initial development are best taken from the Development Plan itself and were, originally, presented as a set of four propositions:-

  (1) that the University is essentially a society of individuals living and working together for the advancement of learning and the dissemination of knowledge at the highest possible level of intellectual achievement and spiritual aspiration. (It follows) that the University must be housed within a limited compass and that there should be provision for a clear hierarchy of groups from the individual to the whole so that it can have sufficient cohesion to operate as a community.
  (2) that the University must be a meeting place of many different aptitudes, skills and specialisation and that each specialisation must be enriched by the greatest possible contact with the others ... (It follows that) over-riding all is a need for compactness and ease of communications between all the constituent parts. Meeting, both accidental and deliberate, must be provided for by the greatest possible number of intersections en route.
  (3) that provision for easy growth and flexibility of use is vital ... the accelerating rate of discovery in many fields of knowledge, particularly in the physical, biological and social sciences which are tending to coalesce and overlap as the conventional boundaries between them have less meaning ... (mean that) it is certain that the design and environment of many of (the University) buildings must permit, and even positively encourage, growth and change.
  (4) that the University community should be provided with particular qualities of environment if the experience of belonging

Introduction

> to it ... is to have for its members the significance and value that it should. (It follows that) in order to meet this tremendous challenge it is necessary to try to discover the characteristic forms and necessary relationships of the buildings in their setting which correspond to the academic and social ideals of the University on the one hand, and to the social and geographic context of the York district on the other. (p. 13)

The extent to which these principles were implemented can be seen in the plan of the University campus (Figure 1). This represents the present stage of growth and development and, unless significant changes in government policies towards universities are made, also reflects the limit of foreseeable development. Small-scale additions are still being made, though, and in recent years two new departments - of archaeology and electronics - have been introduced. However, it does seem likely that the present state of the University will remain substantially unchanged, both physically and academically, for some considerable time.

One thing should stand out from examination of the site plan - that many of the above principles can be seen to have been implemented with singular clarity and achievement. There has been a period of rapid and continuous growth - albeit now at an end - and during this period the University has remained essentially housed within a limited compass while staying coherent and connected. Opportunities for multifarious meetings are evident and available. Relationships between buildings correspond to the principles of the initial academic and social ideals. The present situation, then, twenty years after the publication of the Development Plan, indicates that what was envisaged has largely come about, as the current University Prospectus makes plain :

> The University of York is a collegiate university. The colleges, while avoiding some of the complexities of the traditional collegiate system, are designed both to bridge departmental boundaries and to give the student a centre of loyalty smaller than the whole University. Every member of the University, whether student or staff, is also a member of a college and may reside

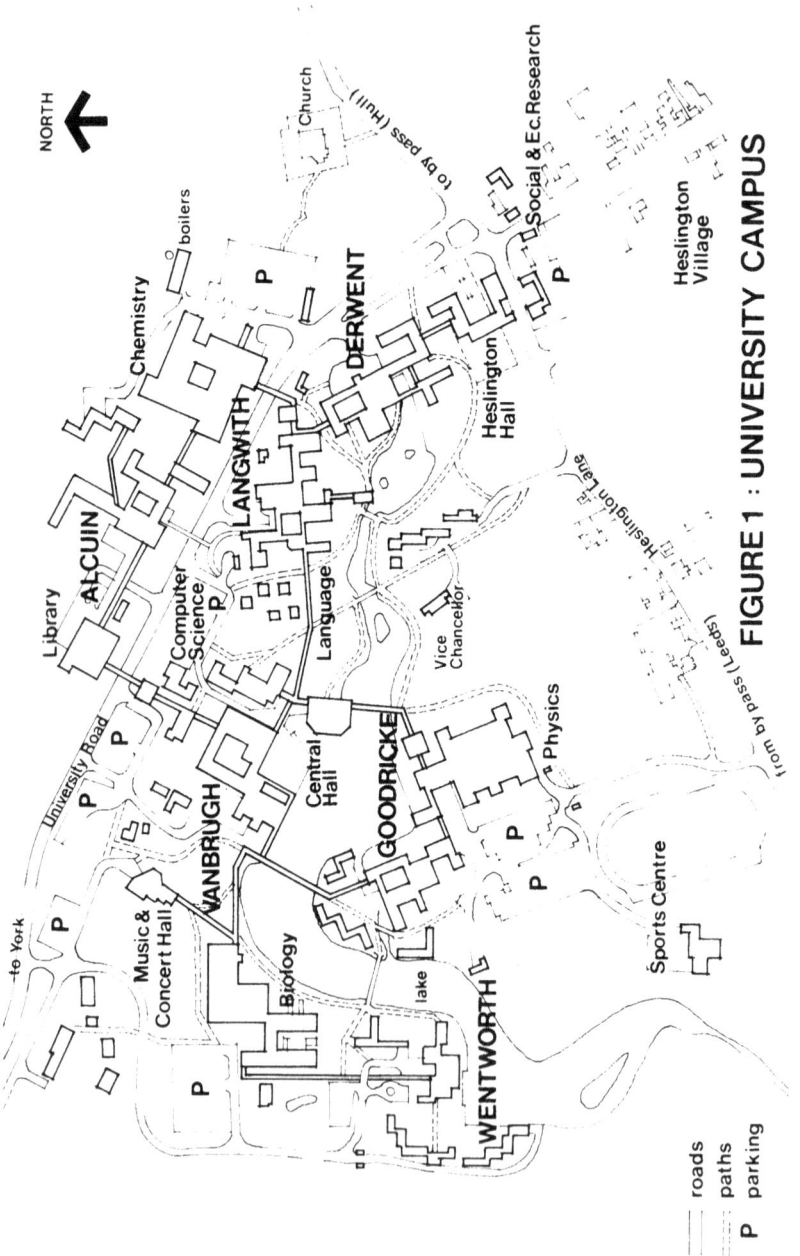

FIGURE 1 : UNIVERSITY CAMPUS

Introduction

there. As well as residential accommodation, the colleges include academic staff offices and lecture and seminar rooms. To a considerable extent therefore living, learning and social life are all centred within the colleges (p. 10)

Whether because of its situation - "York is one of the most beautiful cities in Britain, with fine buildings of many periods, a good river and rich unspoiled countryside close at hand." (ibid. p. 11) - or because of the philosophy outlined above, or because of the academic reputation of its departments, the University undoubtedly attracts a very large number of applicants for its undergraduate courses each year (cf. Heap, 1983, for a current comparison of entry rates and qualifications for all universities).

Specific figures for the latest intake, in terms of entry qualifications are provided in the University Admissions Report (1982). "For the academic year beginning 1981, the University received 12147 applications for an admissions quota of 958 places. This represented an increase of 3.7% compared with the previous year, when the national figure for all applications to universities fell by 0.7%." York places great stress on personal contact with potential students and, of the above 12147 applicants, 7125 interviews were arranged and a further 1081 individual or group visits were offered to applicants who had been made conditional offers. In terms of A level performance, the average A level score for the 986 students who eventually entered the University in 1981 (counting an A grade as 5, down to an E grade as 1) was 11.6 - a figure which has risen steadily over the years.

The following Tables provide a statistical summary of that year's intake to help round out this aspect of the picture of the University.

Table 1.1 Gender Balance (percentages)

	Male	Female
York	57.2	42.8
National*	59.6	40.4

(* Source : UCCA, 1982)

Introduction

Table 1.2 Age Range of York Entrants

Age	-18	18	19	20	21	22	23	24	24+
Number	13	524	303	62	19	14	12	2	37
% of Total	1.3	53.2	30.7	6.3	1.9	1.4	1.2	0.2	3.8

Table 1.3 Choice of York (using UCCA entries in which candidates indicate their preferences in order. It should be noted that it is always difficult to interpret this evidence unambiguously.)

Choice	1	2	3	4	5	CAP*	Clearing**
Number	308	286	173	64	54	6	5
% of Total	40.4	29.0	17.5	6.5	5.5	0.6	0.5

(*CAP = Continuing Applications Procedure.
** Clearing = use of Clearing Scheme during Summer Vacation)

Table 1.4 Regional Distribution of Entrants

Area	Number	% of Total
North	279	28.3
Midlands	175	17.7
South-East	405	41.2
South-West	88	8.9
Scotland	11	1.1
Wales	9	0.9
Ireland	7	0.7
Overseas	12	1.2

Table 1.5 Entrants' Previous Institution

Institution	Number	% of Total
Grammar School	117	11.9
Comprehensive	497	50.4
Independent	203	20.6
Direct Grant	20	2.0
Technical College or College of Further Education	125	12.7
Others	24	2.4

Introduction

   Summarising the above data indicates that undergraduates at York represent a wide range of previous educational backgrounds, with traditional academic institutions providing a significant proportion - although it should be noted that the entry from the private sector of schooling has fallen substantially since the University opened. These undergraduates come from a geographically widespread area, with the vast majority - as with most universities - coming from other parts of the country than the immediate surrounding region. The normative mode of entry is direct from school after completion of a traditional 3 A level course with good grades. There is, however, a tiny minority - slowly growing - of 'mature' students who have broken this traditional pattern by deferring entry and gaining other than school experience before entry. Nearly 90% of entrants had put York within their first three choices of possible university.
   It will be for others to examine the consequences of the outline picture which the above data provides. The extent to which they illustrate features common to many universities, or whether they indicate some special features of York, is obviously important in the context of the later chapters of this book. As has already been indicated, the stance adopted is one which supports the idea of generalising beyond the confines of York to universities as a whole for many aspects of the student experience which we shall examine.
   Some differences which mark York out when compared with other universities can, however, be noted briefly here. It is, of course, a relatively small university. Larger universities will contain more students and more departments and may also operate with different systems of government and academic organisation (Moodie and Eustace (1974) have examined the wide variety of approaches to university government) but York operates with the following structure: there are eighteen departments and no faculties. Teaching and examinations are governed by a Board of Studies in each department, with combined Boards representing each department cooperating in a combined degree. All degrees are Honours Degrees, and students can choose a single subject programme or else a combined degree in which two subjects are offered either in equal combinations or else on a major:minor basis. Boards of Studies are subject to two University academic boards - the Professorial Board, which is nonelective, and the General Academic Board elected by

Introduction

the academic staff from among themselves, together with undergraduates and graduate representatives elected by the student body. These two Boards are answerable, through the University Council - the main executive body - to the supreme governing body of the University, the Court.

Relatively few universities, outside Oxford and Cambridge, have any kind of collegiate structure comparable with that which York has developed. For many universities there is also a lack of residential accommodation on the scale available at York - about 60% of students can live on campus - and such accommodation is frequently found at some distance from the academic centre of the university. The lack of any degree courses other than at an Honours level - although degrees at lower levels are awarded on the basis of a student's final performance - is also a feature which is not common to many universities and may contribute to the relatively high level of entry requirement demanded at York.

The significant opportunities for staff-student co-operation and contact beyond the confines of formal classes - already identified in the Development Plan and illustrated on the Site Plan - and the lack of central social facilities - since each college contains bars, snack bars and dining rooms - are further features which differentiate York from other universities. There are bound to be many other differences which readers familiar with other universities can pin-point, but the above list should indicate an awareness of a number of factors which might limit any later generalisation.

A brief note of elaboration on the colleges will conclude this short account of the University of York. The original Development Plan envisaged a total of eight colleges by the early 1970s. Various changes in government financing have restricted this programme to the current six colleges. The original plan also envisaged that "In the first instance all members of a college will be of the same sex - at least as far as undergraduates are concerned," (ibid. p. 9), and this is certainly no longer the case. Each college is, in effect, intended as a microcosm of the University with subjects, ages, stages and genders of students mixed in broadly the same proportions as they are represented in the University as a whole. Each college is self-governing in many respects, but student entry remains the preserve of individual

Introduction

departments. In addition, and with the exception of the science departments, each college houses two or three academic departments and teaching accommodation. With the social facilities which each college contains there exists, therefore, a range of social and academic meeting places for both formal and informal contact between staff and students. Students are also able to cater for themselves, as each residential corridor contains a small kitchen and eating area.

Colleges, also, through their Junior Common Room Committees, arrange a variety of events throughout the year - from initial welcoming parties for new students through to large-scale concerts open to the rest of the University and, on many occasions to the general public. There is a separate Students Union, affiliated to the NUS, designed to represent the wider situation of students and under this umbrella, independently of the colleges, there is the normal range of student societies and groups which provide additional opportunities for social and recreational contact. College sport flourishes side by side with University sport, and individual interests are also catered for in a central Sports Centre complex.

For each student there is an opportunity for two years of campus residence and immediate proximity with college and departmental contacts. The City of York is within easy reach and provides an alternative source of accommodation of various kinds as well as opportunities for social contact beyond the University. As a further indication of its concern for student well-being, the University is also involved in a number of housing schemes in the area through which yet further sources of accommodation are available. Unlike many of the larger civic universities, accommodation is not a significant problem for students coming to York - whether they wish to live on or off the campus.

There are, therefore, a number of differences within the social dimension of university experience at York when compared with many other British universities. In an academic sense, though, there is every reason to believe that York is comparable with any other university offering similar courses.

Much more could obviously be said to add to this description of the University, but it is hoped that enough has been presented to allow any reader unfamiliar with York to feel that they have a reasonable picture both of the original intentions of the planners and also of how these plans have

Introduction

developed to the present time. As an indication of how resilient were the ideas of the original planners it is worth noting here that the University of York has escaped relatively lightly from the cuts imposed within the university sector by the UGC in its implementation of government policy in the early 1980s.

    York, then, is a university designed to promote good staff-student relationships at many levels. The studies which form the basis for the following chapters should, therefore, have been expected to produce findings which are part of the everyday stock of knowledge of members of the University. What each of them does, however, make clear is that, in spite of physical arrangements and administrative intentions, the experiences of students at York are not at all straightforward. In many cases it would appear that the actuality perceived by the students runs counter to the official perspectives which staff put forward.

Chapter 2

BECOMING A STUDENT

(Researched by Victoria Billington)

Going up to university (the phrase itself reflects the conventional regard that such a move is towards a higher, more elevated position) must surely be considered one of the most important steps in a person's life. When I began my own undergraduate career in October 1974, I anticipated the event as heralding many exciting challenges and new opportunities. I recognised that there would naturally be difficulties to overcome in acclimatising to any new environment but was not preoccupied with these.

Consequently, when I decided to research into the plight of new students, at the beginning of my third year, I did not set out with any assumptions concerning the nature of the problems which might confront them or ways in which they might be surmounted. I aimed to take the role of participant observer, to observe and present what Becker (1968) refers to as a "natural history" of events and conditions and the reactions of new students to what they encountered: to record what is entailed in "becoming a student". I was not looking for subjects simply for their relevance to empirical confirmation of certain hypotheses by observation, so I had constantly to beware of ascribing typical motives or of constructing typical patterns of behaviour.

According to Bierstedt (1957), norms refer to ways of "doing" as opposed to ways of "thinking". Social order is therefore synonymous with the existences of norms, although one is seldom aware of them until they are violated or until an attempt is made to enter a new environment where one is trying to establish oneself. A new student approaches his role-taking situation with a background of conventions or ignorance, for he has as yet no knowledge of his own experiencing to draw upon. As a student myself, I was automatically still part of the context I wished to observe, but armed with two years of my own experiences, and those of my friends and acquaintances, I could use these to form a firm foundation for the "sensitising process" which is the most important factor in the self-orientation of any observer.

Because of the study I was undertaking, however, I was no longer taking my "normal" role in the society but was participating in it on what Schwartz and Schwartz (1955) call the "simply human level" and, in addition, the "planned role level", that is both as a "native" of the environment, and as a scientific observer who was already on the "inside". (Indeed, I even lived in a hall of residence.) I aimed at what Wieder (1974) has called "telling the code", to exhibit rather than explain the work members of society do to sustain a social order. While my personal circumstances greatly facilitated this, they will also have limited or biassed situations to an unquantifiable extent, for I was part of the code, disturbing situations, making my own personal impact and therefore influencing the people and situations observed.

Much literature arises from the increasing interest in productivity in higher education. It is frequently misconceived because it stems from a wanting to analyse failure, which is generally assumed to be failure to complete a course and gain a degree. (It does not assume any other gains may be derived from the time employed.) Also, the vast majority of surveys employ data which are derived from questionnaire-based techniques and are neatly quantifiable for presentation. In contrast, the seemingly mundane things I recorded may seem obvious when written down but can provide great insight, for example into the nature of what Cicourel (1964) has described as the "tickets" which people use to start conversations. The aim of my study was not to be that its readers could exclaim 'That's true, but I'd never noticed it before' or 'That's just how I remember it', prolonging the attitude expressed by second and third year students sitting complacently surrounded by friends observing new entrants on their first evening, "Thank God _I_ haven't got to go through that again", and that the matter should end there. But this recognition and acknowledgement is a necessary stage on the way towards facilitating the transition into "studenthood" in ways which may possibly have been previously overlooked because of

Becoming a Student

failure to see the situation of first year students as it is in reality.
It is easy to forget that the new student meets a bewildering set of experiences which demand a variety of new social competences. Looking down from the "advanced" position of a second or third year onto the new students' fumbling attempts at adapting to the "superior" norms of behaviour of the higher years, it is easy and convenient to forget how you reacted when not recognising one familiar face in a crowded room, and when the only knowledge you had of the place was derived from the prospectus, teachers or friends. Knowledge of the environment the new student aspires to belong to is, for the most part, socially derived from others. He/she must trust, accept and rely upon definitions interpreted from those already in the environment to help in dealing with situations which are potentially problematic, and for which there are no explicit rules.
Wieder (1974) has suggested that "The code, then, is much more a method of moral persuasion and justification than it is a substantive account of an organised way of life ... the same explanatory and descriptive utterances often are, and always can be, sanctions, justifications, or urgings of some course of action in the relationship between hearer and speaker," (p. 158).
It is therefore essential to remember that whoever teaches this code may well be motivated to formulate it in his or her own interests. Though no rules could be written down that say "you will get drunk a lot at university" (or vice versa), "you will not do much academic work at university" (or vice versa), such activities portray relatively clear indications as to the directions in which one's loyalties lie. Models of what is appropriate and expected of new students are derived from two sets of stimuli: the students and the staff of the university, and these are often in conflict.
On arrival at university, the new student must, as Miller (1970) puts it, "find his way through what may seem an amorphous body of information and try to synthesize where synthesis is not apparent." (p. 72) This body of information is presented in countless ways, from the casual verbal remark to the formal documents distributed by the university authorities. At the beginning of the academic year 1976-77, I tried to re-enter the situation of the new student: I collected all the literature and attended phrenetically all the events the new stu-

dents are expected to in my efforts to study this assault of information and observe how the cultural norms (which include culturally approved goals and the means for their attainment) are learned and shared.

The first week of one's university life can make or break a career there, for it has its own peculiar features and problems. I felt the general atmosphere among new students could be summed up as "confusion". Ryle (1969) calls it "uncertainty": "it is not surprising that this uncertainty is reflected especially clearly in the thoughts, feelings and actions of an age-group primarily concerned with the search for personal identity," (p. 16). The practical problems of registration, grants, residence, may be pressing at this time, but they do not present as many difficulties as the personal and moral crises involved in adapting to one's role within the university environment. The Professor of Sociology said, in his introductory talk to his new students: "You spend the first five or six days here wondering how on earth you can get into university life, and the rest of your three years wondering how the hell you can get out!" Perhaps this is true.

The first week of the academic year at the university where this study was conducted, is referred to as Week 0 - itself generating a feeling of being in limbo, with nothing much happening. Its alternative title is "Freshers' Week". The term "fresher" is applied to all new students, carrying with it associations of innocence, ignorance, naivity, "greenness" and perhaps implies it is impossible to retain one's "freshness" after this week. It is interesting that the "freshers" themselves do not appear to object to the personal application of the term, but second and third years are very indignant if mistakenly so addressed, considering it to be a very derogatory label.

How does one "spot the fresher"? Older students said it was something about the eyes, the quick nervousness, they blush very easily, are desperately friendly to everyone, read everything on all the noticeboards and stand out by their lonely helpless looks of desperation at discos. In addition, they are often particularly noticeable by the clothes they wear.

Clothing represents a great problem for the student who does not wish to run the risk of being unduly conspicuous. It therefore seems unfair that they should be subjected to misrepresentative

Becoming a Student

advertising such as the posters for the "Freshers' Ball" (alias the "Who's Who Waltz"). These depicted a couple elegantly attired in evening dress dancing, whereas at the "Waltz" most students were inelegantly dressed in jeans or variations on that theme - as the girls who turned up in long formal dresses quickly discovered. The problem did not appear so pressing for the men.

The pervading nervousness among new students exhibits itself in a dread of doing anything wrong and looking foolish. (One I spoke to at an introductory talk said, "The only thing to do is to keep your mouth shut for the first three weeks.") No second year I asked could remember anything said in the College Provost's introductory talk to them except it was long and boring and full of jokes which fell flat. This was hardly surprising from what I observed of one of this year's talks, when all the students seemed more concerned with looking nervously round the room. The common actions they perform, which illustrate this dread, are a kind of "follow my leader". This was particularly noticeable when, after the Provost's talk, all the first years filed down to the Junior Common Room, as they had been asked to do, for the evening's entertainment provided by the Junior Common Room Committee, and started to queue to get into what was an empty room. Although they were told that free beer and cider were available from the serving hatch, it took quite a lot of persuasion, coupled with the example of the few older students, to get them over there.

One girl I spoke to at this event had arrived the previous evening and told me she had woken in the morning and wanted to go to the toilet, but she could hear people talking in the kitchen and she didn't have the courage to leave her room for an hour, even though she knew how stupid she was being. Neither could she face eating in the college dining room as she didn't know what to do with herself or where to sit.

She emphasised for me that what one needs most of all in this strange new environment is courage, especially to face such horrendous first week events as the Freshers' Ball, already mentioned. One older student told me he couldn't imagine a more hostile situation for new students to be in as everyone else seemed to know so many people. It is interesting at such events that it is easy to "spot the second and third years" as well as the freshers. The second years seemed to do everything with more show and gusto than anybody else, from talking to people they knew to dancing, perhaps to demonstrate that they knew the ropes and could now impart their knowledge to a younger year, whereas they had been the "novices" up till then. In contrast, the third years seemed more "mellow" and wrapped up in their own concerns.

Because, at least during the first few days, it is so easy to pick out the new students, it is also easy to observe how and why people establish contact with each other under these circumstances. The majority of opening remarks used to start conversations referred to the mutual plight of the protagonists, such as "Isn't it awful being in a room with all these people you don't know!" A second year student told me he had gone back to his room after fifteen minutes of the Freshers' Disco in his first year because it had been too cramped and he got tired of people asking him what subject he was doing and whereabouts in his block he lived. These are exactly the sort of questions I heard people asking each other constantly. Such questions have become cliches for older students who use them when mimicking the situation of the first years, asking each other what A level grades they have got and where their home towns are.

Another girl I spoke to at the Freshers' Disco asked me if I shared her feelings when I arrived here, that she would never be able to get on with any of the people, yet she had come with the expectation of making so many friends. As an example, she said she had met a first year mathematician, but all he could talk about was how good at maths. he was and all the books he had bought. Consequently she felt that she, a social scientist, would never get on with anyone studying maths. A third year friend of mine told me her first night had been spent dismissing people as possible acquaintances, often just at a first glance, and I got indications that this sort of thing was happening again, especially between people of different disciplines.

The first years seemed to find companionship in adversity, and the groups which formed were predominantly single sex. They were obviously finding it easier to approach members of the same sex. This was in contrast to second and third years who showed their prime interest to be in approaching members of the opposite sex and in trying their luck with the "new talent". Looking at the girls' reticent responses and embarrassed looks when approached by a male student, a lot of them thought "ulterior motives" were the reason for this expression of interest in them. Judging from a remark made by a small group of second or third year males, and aimed at myself and two girl friends standing together at a disco on the very first evening - "She's a first year" (wrong, incidentally, all third years!), "I'd like to fuck that!" - they were not always wrong!

There is a lot of sexual awareness at events such as the introductory discos. Comments from other students, such as, "As soon as I saw that girl with the long blond hair I knew Jimmy would be after her", abounded. These situations must be even more alienating for the men than for the women, at whom most of the attention is directed, even in these "liberated" times. Incidentally, older students who were approached by lecherous members of their own years, in the mistaken belief they were approaching a first year, were very indignant - but more at being thought a "fresher" than because of the lascivious nature of the approach!

Sex takes on increasing prominence in conversations at university. Perhaps it is because it is more easily available through lack of regulations and watchful guardians. No doubt for some this is shocking and embarrassing, at least at first. The same may be true of alcohol. It is notable that at the first social events a lot of new students got drunk very quickly, especially the girls. This may be due to heightened nervous excitement, or perhaps because they are unused to drinking.

In both the college introductory talk by the Chairperson of the Junior Common Room Committee, and the Students' Union Forum, a great deal of emphasis was placed on the number of bars on the campus and on drinking "events". Older students constantly stress the bravado of the drunkard and recount with glee the more colourful antics of the various university "piss-artists". It was interesting to observe the new students beginning to talk of how drunk they had been on various occasions since their arrival, especially when looking back on their first week.

Drunken cavortings were only a further example of the stress second and third year students placed on the unacademic side of university life. They also made points of stressing the anti-academic side. For example, the Junior Common Room Committee Chairperson addressing new students on their first night told them not to ask him where the college library is as he had been there for two years and still not found it. The Deputy President of the Students' Union informed the assembled congregation that no-one would need to go to the main library very often so he would not tell them how to find it. (The Central University Library is, incidentally, referred to affectionately as "the snack bar in the sky", due to its position on a hill.)

Another, very forceful, frontal attack is launched on the new students in the political field. Although they may not have given much consideration to the political side of university life, this was forced upon them early in the first week of term. The campus was swamped with leaflets - they were even delivered around individual rooms in residence blocks - <u>demanding</u> student attendance at union meetings, telling them how they <u>ought</u> to feel about such issues as gay liberation and the anti-apartheid campaign: there was even a picket line outside the local branch of Barclay's Bank in protest at that bank's South African interests, aimed at preventing new students from opening accounts there. At the doors of the Vice-Chancellor's formal welcome gathering on the Wednesday morning, the first fully organised day of the week, leaflets from all political parties represented at the University were thrust at the students. The bluntest example of political conflict within the University was in the International Socialists' handout presented at this occasion. This warned of the two faces of the then Vice-Chancellor in rather crude and personal terms.

Incidentally, all the official representatives of the University introduced, and the excellent advice given by the Vice-Chancellor on this occasion, were not remembered at all by the students I mentioned it to afterwards. All they could recall was that he had asked individuals or groups to invite him to tea as he enjoyed meeting students. The general consensus of opinion was that no-one would dare to invite him as they wouldn't know what to talk about.

Throughout the rest of that Wednesday, many more introductory talks were arranged for the new students, one being presented by each academic department. Joint course students experienced more trouble with regard to these, as many were not sure whether to attend the talks in all departments their course would be concerned with. This was particularly pertinent for students on a new combined subject course, being run for the first time that year, for they seemed to have been forgotten about by both departments.

Becoming a Student

Before one of these talks started, one girl in the audience turned round and asked generally how much reading people had done and how many books they had bought, (I later learned that many students had bought all the books on their reading lists) presumably dreading the thought, or wanting verification, that she had done more or less than anybody else. The tutor who openend this talk advised the students to "give it a try and don't go home to Mum". He also said that what one gets out of university courses is related to what one puts into them and, in addition, that the students should avoid becoming distracted from the exiting intellectual experience of university by worrying about the economic difficulties of such institutions. (I must admit that this was the first time I had heard such a reason given for possible distraction from academic work at this stage of one's career.) The most outstanding remark, in my opinion and perhaps reflecting a senior student's perspective, was when one of the tutors said he considered the literature sent out by the University saying "what is a seminar" unnecessary, for if the students could not find out for themselves pretty quickly, they should not be there. After such comments, he went on to say "Don't let people alienate you here"!
    I talked to one girl after yet another departmental talk in the afternoon, and she told me she had found the whole day rather strange and confusing. She had been to lots of talks and accumulated an absolute plethora of paper. Each talk she felt to be simply another on a never-ending line, none of them saying anything different. Of course, each one had been different, and different people and different information would have been presented, but presumably she had just become numbed to them.
    The main introductory talk arranged by the students themselves for all the first years was also held later in the same afternoon. It was hardly surprising that, by that stage in the day, not very many were present, especially when contrasted with the numbers at the Vice-Chancellor's talk first thing in the morning. Introductory talks are all very well, but the danger of overdoing things was clearly demonstrated when the President of the Students' Union informed the students that he planned to break from the introductory speeches for about an hour to show a film made by the World in Action team. This was to launch the union's campaign against apartheid in South Africa which, he told everyone, the University feels very strongly about. Many

people left when they heard what the meeting was to be about, and many more left when the time for the film drew near. Clearly their own priorities at this time lay elsewhere.

That evening the Freshers' Ball, already mentioned, was held. It is hardly surprising that the following day many students said they had had to leave the dance early because they were so tired. By this stage in the week exhaustion was the main affliction from which we were all suffering.

In contrast to the intense activities of Wednesday, the rest of the week presented problems for some of the new students as to how they were to fill in their days once they had registered and seen their supervisors. Many people asked me the way to the Book-Mart and to Co-op, an informal chat/ counselling organisation. Some I spoke to had arrived on the previous Sunday or Monday, either to benefit from a lift with their parents (one girl described her parents as her "life-line") or to get the administrative functions finished early. They had not realised it was not possible to begin registration etc. until the Wednesday, and there was nothing arranged for them to do once they had been given their handouts.

By the weekend, all the new students seemed exhausted and several I spoke to were longing for the first "real" week to begin, with the start of their courses. This was in contrast to two girls I met a few days into term who said they were still waiting for something to happen and to meet lots of people (expressing a similar attitude to two boys I overhead outside a disco in the first week: "Well, there's nothing happening in there."). This raised for me the question of what exactly they expect to "happen" to them in terms of the University Experience. It may be interesting to cite here a tutor's anticipation of this quoted by Miller (1970): "Iliffe at Keele cites Professor Mansfield Cooper as saying "Students come up to university with little sense of obligation and a sharp sense of rights ... the common complaint is that a lecture has not been interesting ... the student expects as of right, to be interested,"" (p. 127). Purely by chance, I learnt that one of these girls left the University at the beginning of her second term. Perhaps the "big moment" she had been waiting for never materialised.

Towards the end of Week 0 the new students were demonstrating greater confidence in social situations, for example at a disco several of them were now dancing in groups and appeared to be enjoying the organised competitions, though did not actually join in any. Although very few events were arranged solely for the first years after the first week, it was possible to monitor their progress under other circumstances and to observe how they continue to establish themselves.

The mixed distribution of rooms on each corridor across the years (enforced by the college in its room allocations) clearly facilitates the broadening of experience and circles of acquaintance, though initially the first years said they would prefer to have been all together. (They seemed to find it easier to talk amonst themselves, especially about blunders that they had made, and were sometimes embarrassed if older students overheard this evidence of ignorance and mistakes.) This integration gives them a chance to see other students in easier situations. One of the new students on my corridor, for example, said she was glad I was having problems writing essays as she thought I looked so confident and in control. She thought it was only the first years who were experiencing difficulties - which may, after all, be what a lot of people unconsciously or consciously set out to make her think. (It is very easy to get such a superficial view of others which may make oneself feel incomptetent or inadequate, for example in a library it is easy to think that everyone else is working hard and learning a lot when in fact many of them may be simply sitting over their books, as Blackie and Gowenlock (1964) have indicated.)

Apart from those living near each other, it is interesting to see which students find an easy entree into the community. What it is that makes them welcome with open arms, or else finds ranks very firmly closed against them. People who wish to become affiliated to the close-knit societies such as the Christian Union or Gaysoc find it easier to get together, as do those from the same home town and those who are good at some form of sport such as football. (Drinking is also classed as a "sport" and the same thing applies.) These are all areas in which it is comparatively easy to define oneself and to become accepted.

One can also consider whether or not the majority of new students are primarily interested in getting to know other new students as they will be together longer, or whether it makes no difference at all. Some seemed intent on getting to know second or third years, often on a boyfriend/girlfriend basis. But often, I learnt from talking to my own acquaintances, new students go out with older students for the first few weeks, and are introduced to all their friends, then the relationship breaks up and suddenly the new student is back to square one, not knowing anyone in his or her own year. Or, indeed, they may be in an even worse position as by then lots of initial groups and cliques have already formed and which can be very difficult to infiltrate.

In addition to getting to know other students, several first years seem particularly keen to get onto committees and such like. At the beginning of the first term two new students stood for election onto the College Council, and were both elected unopposed. If there had been other candidates (and it is interesting in itself that there were not) I feel their chances of election would have been greatly reduced, for at such an early stage in their university careers it must be impossible for them to realise fully the functions of the post they stood for and the roles they must fulfill in order to do the jobs efficiently. I later asked one of the girls concerned why she had stood for election, and she told me that although she had no real idea of what was involved she hoped to learn about the college through sitting on the committee. However, she subsequently found it not exciting enough for her and she was not going to stand for re-election at Christmas. Interestingly, both girls then went on to take part in activities and posts connected with the central Students' Union instead.

The Provost's Wine Parties, which he had mentioned in his welcoming talk, took place throughout the first few weeks of the term. At one of these I spoke to a couple of new students who had taken a year off before coming to university. They were quite cocky about this, feeling it put them at an advantage over students who had come straight from school. I also spoke to a new mature student and he too was much more self-assured than the majority, asking about the music scene and other specific aspects of university life which interested him. We went for a drink in the college bar and he offered to buy the barmaids a drink. They told him they were completely unused to such courtesy and said that most students, especially first years, usually don't even say "please" and "thank you" when they order drinks. (Though in one college there is a barmaid who will not serve anybody unless they do so.) This emphasised that it is not only their peers that new students have to learn to get on with; the porters, cleaners, barmaids, bursars, etc. also have their vital roles to play.

Topics of conversation between students also changed as the term got under way. Much discussion of the price of food in the shops and in the dining rooms emphasised how unaware of such matters the student is who has come straight from home. Some of them expressed themselves to be very wary of spending money, whereas some were decidedly extravagant: it is more than likely the first time most students have had total control over their own finances. The "coffee rounds" had started early in the first week with students reporting how many visitors they had had for coffee at any one time. They also often said how late they had stayed up talking, which they enjoyed tremendously: close relationships and profound late-night discussions appear to be romantic preconceptions of university life.

Chance remarks from conversations with older students can give cause for concern to the new student who is still unsure of the new environment. For example, a first year boy I knew had met a third year girl who told him she was going to choose his room to live in for the year, but had decided against it. He then became very concerned that there was something wrong with it, especially in the light of rumours from other students who were always keen to spread the idea that some rooms in college were haunted. Other remarks overhead, such as, "It's dead here at weekends", run the risk of becoming self-fulfilling prophecies.

As the term progressed and the new students began to settle down and make friends, it was interesting to hear that second and third years were feeling that the friendly atmosphere they were used to in such places as the college bar had gone, as there were lots of "strangers" around. In such a moving environment, older students also have to adapt to the changing social situations such as occur when they lose friends and co-students into the world of graduates.

As different close-knit groups of friends become noticeably established, those who have not found a niche so easily may begin to worry about where they fit in. One new student I came across in the kitchen late one night said he was finding it very difficult to get on with people, for he felt he needed a few friends to form close personal relationships with, whereas everyone else seemed to favour the more general society of large groups. He said he was depressed and confused and was having trouble sleeping as a result. He was experiencing difficulties not only in finding direction in his personal life, but also in his academic work. He said he couldn't find a central point in his course. He felt students were split, as tutors urged them to "do their own things" academically, yet also decreed very close lines to work within.

In addition, he told me he had met a mature student on his course who had been living in Bahrein and they had discussed the political situation out there. He had enjoyed the discussion very much, but it had served to increase his belief that he had nothing to offer in seminar discussions, in contrast to people such as this mature student and the tutors who had experienced and read so much.

This disillusionment and lack of self-confidence was notable amongst many new students as they attended their "first" lecture and "first" seminar. Many of them found seminars cause for worry instead of being the exciting intellectual challenges they had been led to believe. One girl told me she couldn't say anything in her tutorials, which just served to make her feel stupid and intellectually inferior. She described herself as not really the sort of person to talk in these situations (which surprised me as she is very chatty normally), but acknowledged that discussion is the main point of tutorials and seminars. (This recalled for me the time I attended an "open" seminar conducted by F.R. Leavis: he announced that as we were all undergraduates he did not consider it worthwhile having a discussion with us, so he read us a poem, told us how he had had tea with T.S. Eliot, and sent us packing.)

On the train south in the second weekend in November, I sat opposite a boy and a girl who were both getting off about half an hour down the line. The girl said she had <u>only</u> been home once this term, and that people she knew who had the furthest to travel (to London and beyond) went home the most frequently. They were both reeling off all the people in their home town who were getting engaged or married, and also describing long lists of new acquaintances made at university, demonstrating how many they knew. The girl said how good it was to be going home again, speaking as if she had been away on an epic voyage. One of the most notable features about them was that he was wearing a striped University scarf, and she was wearing a sweat shirt with the University emblem emblazoned on it: consequently, they were both instantly recognisable as students. They also started grinning at me very amicably when I produced my student railcard for the guard, and they could see I was also a student. This experience made me think that perhaps going home to familiar faces and surroundings where one can recount as many experiences of university life as one chooses, may be one of the most important ways to strengthen the recognition that one is a student.

One of the underlying areas of interest throughout my research concerned the reasons why people even go to university, for these obviously go hand in hand with their expectations - wherever these originate and however they are met. Do students expect to emerge with an automatic "place in society", to step into an interesting job with a high salary? Popular cliches are that university is seen as an escape from "reality" for both students and tutors; as ivory tower institutions where irrelevant knowledge is pursued for its own irrelevant ends; as glorified holiday camps with backstage suffering.

Universities are aware that students choose them for many reasons other than the academic content of their courses. On occasions, students cited to me their reasons for selecting this particular university as being that it was not too far from their home; that their choice of subject was decreed by what they were best at in school; that the chosen course did not sound as if it had too much hard work; that they thought a university degree would be more prestigious than that to be gained in alternative forms of higher education which they had been offered. One girl told me she had put this University on her UCCA form in first, second and fifth place, each time for a different subject: she said she didn't care what she studied as long as it was here.

Another student I spoke to said he had come to university to break from the definition he felt was being created for him by his family and friends, so that he could establish a new identity.

Douglas (1964), in a study at the London School of Economics, found that many students looked on their undergraduate years as a moratorium, an interim period when they hoped to "find themselves" and their relation to the world, and to give them time to decide what they wanted to become by postponing the necessity for taking such decisions. I also found this to be a notable characteristic of undergraduates at this university - even halfwway through their final year, very few had given serious thought to "what comes next".

Reasons for leaving university prior to the completion of one's course are often closely linked to those for coming in the first place. One female student I spoke to was just leaving the University after six weeks. She said she felt that university was for the young to find themselves or else for older-minded people's education in a more academic than personal sense. (Iliffe (1969) would agree with her: "Reading for a degree and growing up are tasks which some people find they can only tackle consecutively, and not concurrently.") She left because she felt she had already had a strong sense of her own identity, and now realised the sort of education she saw the University to be providing was not what she needed or wanted for herself.

All the literature which deals with life at university acknowledges certain difficulties that students encounter, and draws a parallel with the transition from Primary to Secondary School, from being a big fish in a small pond to a small fish in a big pond. Advice and suggestions are given in the light of such difficulties, such as that a year off between school and university may be very valuable in helping the student determine more clearly his or her purpose in entering higher education. Miller (1970), for example, feels that a year in industry or other work would be a good test of motivation to pursue an academic career or discipline, and George Bernard Shaw (1914) decided: "What is the matter with our universities is that the students are school-children, whereas it is of the very essence of university education that they should be adults ... if our universities would exclude everybody who had not earned a living by his or her own exertions for at least a couple of years, their effect would be vastly improved." (p. xli)

Fields in which research is required are also features of this literature. Several emphasise the ways in which pupils are prepared at school as an example of the wrong expectations which may be inculcated in students. For instance, if pupils are over-crammed and specifically directed towards qualifying exams, they may find difficultiy in adjusting from mechanical to broader methods of study. Miller (1970) cites Carr-Saunders, who "made the point that whereas success at the university depends upon exploring interest, wide-ranging curiosity and initiative, the exams on which selection to university is based, tend to over-emphasise capacity for absorption," (p. 187). One must also consider to what extent his criteria for success are true ones.

Are universities being completely honest to those who apply to enter the hallowed sanctuaries in the image they portray of themselves? Such considerations indicate the need for them to interpret themselves better to their students, before and after arrival, even if this entails an admission of the confusion concerning their own aims and expectations. No-one denies that a university prospectus is a "sales brochure" designed to attract, but it does give rise to questionable expectations.

In the year this study was conducted, the Students' Union, following the example of other universities, tried to produce an "alternative" prospectus. The aims of this prospectus were to give views on the courses, the pros and cons of a campus university, the benefits or disadvantages of a year off, and so forth. Such information would clearly be most interesting and valuable for potential students to consider alongside the official versions. However, the response to questionnaires for background information for the first edition was not large. Perhaps this was a further indication of the "I'm alright Jack" attitude of students already established, or that many are reasonably content. All the questions on the sheet were posed with the supposition that a lot was wrong. The voice that replies "none" to the question "What major changes would you like to see? (e.g. range of course, teaching methods)" is not very likely to get heard. But at least if as many cases as possible are presented to the new students, conflicts apparent on arrival may not be so surprising.

But while students are battling ahead stressing the anti-academic side of university, (even in the alternative prospectus Physics is advocated as "Practicals can be fun with the chance of a long morning coffee break and an early finish in the afternoon") the University authorities forge away stressing the formal benefits and academic privileges to be derived. It is hardly surprising that disillusionment with both sides can set in when conflicting claims and demands begin to exert pressure. Many students find it almost impossible to balance all these and may not even recognise the ultimate coup de grace is to leave university with a brilliant degree, while never having been seen to do any academic work at all.

The main problem of university life is the "embarras de richesse". There is an absolute plethora of people to meet, things to do and see, and so much to learn. Once the University has attracted and accepted its annual intake of students, it sends them booklets to provide them with information about many of these activities and advice on how to cope. One from the authorities - "Studying at the University,,.", which tells how to make use of hours between lectures, etc. - one from the Students' Union - "Life at University", which informs you of such facts as that you might find the Book Mart useful "if you read books". Another guidebook recommended is Blackie and Gowenlock's (1964) revision of Truscott's (1946) introduction to the first year at university, but the tone of this is so unbearably moral and didactic that the useful bits of advice and information get overlooked. Guidebooks do have a role to play in preparing students for university, but many students I spoke to about them have never read them (or say that they haven't), and those that have done so say that although they know (after some time at university) all that they have to tell them, it is always putting the advice into practice that presents the problem.

The need to feel that you have someone to turn to for advice and assistance with personal and/or academic problems, instead of just the guidebooks, is vital in a university career where role transactions are occurring in rapid succession. Holbech (1967), when discussing the findings of his enquiry into the problems of transition from school to university, expressed the opinion that universities should take more interest in the academic life of their students. This, he argued, would give the students some sense of identity and a feeling that they are "wanted" members of the academic community, which would do much to counteract their personal problems. I would agree with him.

This university places much emphasis on its supervisory system, with specific tutors being allocated a number of students each year. However, this system takes effort on both sides to work and to be worthwhile. All the University literature stressed that you should take any worries to your tutor, but students from all years (especially in the social sciences) complained frequently that they could never get hold of their tutors, or talk to them alone, and they have the impression that the

Becoming a Student

tutors do not care for them at all.
    In contrast, I came across a large queue outside the office of one tutor in the English Department, during the first week of term. The tutor was very behind in the times she had allocated to see her supervisees, but one girl in the queue told me that she is always so interested to talk to them, and always allows each supervisee about half an hour alone with her (many other tutors have group supervisory sessions, or else allow as little time as ten minutes per student), that none of them minded being kept waiting.
    Many conflicting expectations emerged from this study, particularly concerning staff/student relationships. However much the University may stress the great rapport which exists, it is often difficult to acknowledge its presence in practice (though this must be a difficult matter, as it is generally individual personalities which create any problems). Perhaps it would be a worthwhile exercise for both staff and students to express what they expect from each other and why, either verbally or in writing. No doubt all concerned would be amazed at the discrepancies between them, but at least each might come to recognise the other's difficulties, and adapt accordingly.
    Any efforts to make informal staff/student contact, such as drinking or dining together, should also be encouraged, for in such ways people could also learn more about each other which could not fail to amend any initial and perhaps prejudiced feelings about "them" and "us" into something at least founded on experience. Although the Vice-Chancellor stressed that the University is founded on fellow scholarship, how many students feel they can sit "beside" their tutors in the learning process instead of "under" them - and how many tutors would want then to feel this anyway?
    It is essential to stress that the University does in fact do a great deal to help incoming students. In this respect, the advantages of a collegiate system become manifest, bringing the new community down to a more manageable size. However, the arrangements made are appropriate for the ways in which the Vice-Chancellor, the tutors, the Students' Union, etc. view the problems, requirements and opportunities connected with this period of transition and adjustment, and it became clear throughout the course of my investigation that these were not always the correct ones in the circumstances. For example, the Students' Union had

clearly felt that the Introductory Forum was the
ideal place to channel the interests and energies
of the new students into the anti-apartheid campaign, but this was particularly misplaced and badly
timed. New students can only take a certain amount
of information, and assaults on their emotions, and
the launching of this campaign probably alienated
people instead of attracting them

In contrast to this, several students mentioned
to me how surprised and pleased they had been to
receive visits or invitations to tea from older
students studying the same subject, or being members of the same societies. They had benefited
from the visit themselves and also from knowing that
other students had taken the trouble to get in
touch. (Though one English student was worried that
an invitation she had received to tea might have
been some kind of "Christian recruitment" in disguise!)

Iliffe (1969) suggested that seventeen-year-old school-children's hopes and expectations from
university were very important features to be considered when planning university courses and policies
and that research into these "powerful consumers"
was very necessary. Such research is, of course,
now under way under the direction of Professor
Gareth Williams at Lancaster and Professor Maurice
Kogan at Brunel.

Another area in which I came to feel that research was desperately needed was the policy of
taking a year off, and an attempt at determining
the effects on students' motivations and expectations. Everything possible must be done to help
all students to recognise and understand for themselves their reasons for going to university, even
if the motives and hopes behind them were originally their parents' or their teachers', and not
their own, if the experience is to be as valuable
as it can be for each individual. Perhaps, in
addition, such features as the setting up of student "communes" after graduation near the university
attended will then decrease. Whilst this development may be a consequence of changing patterns of
graduate employment, it might also be the case that
such graduates seem to be waiting for something
from the university which they have not yet got from
their years inside it.

Issues concerning the nature and purpose of
universities are constantly being raised, but cannot be discussed often enough. A meeting was advertised at the University on handouts headed "The

Becoming a Student

problem is to learn what learning is for". People were invited to come and discuss "what do you think of your education?", but the whole meeting disintegrated rapidly into a political brawl. It is only through increased investigation and constructive discussion that the education provided can be as full, relevant, complete and beneficial to all as it should be.

For me, this study gave rise to questions on an even broader scale. I now feel it necessary, for example, for everybody to ask themselves if universities, as they are at present, being places where people are all shut up together, many of them still bearing strong attitudes derived from their schooling, are in fact the right sort of environment for advanced academic study. Perhaps, for example, the social life and other distractions are supplied in over-large quantities.

I am aware that it was only while being a student myself, and therefore a part of the life I was attempting to describe, that I could have conducted this kind of study. Perhaps it is only at the end of a university career that you come to realise "what it's all about", and then you wish you could go back and do it again properly! This study emphasised for me the need for every member of the University to assist others through their own attempts at making sense of the environment.

Perhaps the main requisites to achieving this greater mutual knowledge - and consequent understanding between the universities and the outside world, between the staff and the students - are honesty, effort and openness on all sides. And this, of course, raises again the question of the extent to which a university, with the clear contrasts between staff and student perspectives, between the institutional and the personal needs of its members, can, realistically, become a real community instead of a collection of often discrete and unconnected small groups. If this process of coming together can be encouraged, then help can naturally be provided to ease the passage of students into and through university life with greater fulfillment.

Chapter 3

IMPLICATIONS OF STUDENTS' USE OF LIBRARIES

(Researched by Ursula Newell)

Much effort and goodwill is expended on providing university sudents with library facilities and instruction - or reader education as it is sometimes called - to enable the best use to be made of these facilities. A brief indication of the comparison between individual universities in respect of library facilities is contained in the Sunday Times (1983), and the annual D.E.S. statistical publications provide yet another source of detail for those interested.
Until recently, reader education has been more concerned with making sure that students use existing library services efficiently than with integrating such services with the students' existing bibliographic skills, or with the precise demands of their courses. It is not that librarians who planned and taught these library instruction programmes were arrogant or unfeeling, but rather that they operated according to their own professional perspective on the role of the library and the choice of information collection methods without realising that academics and students often had different perspectives.
This researcher's original experience in this field came through appointment as a reader services librarian at Melbourne's La Trobe University. Reference to the literature of professional librarianship indicates that the kinds of experiences in an Australian context are universal and not peculiar; that the kinds of attitudes which inform a university librarian's view of the role are reinforced through training and then confirmed in practice. It will be worthwhile ensuring that readers are familiar with the way in which these professional notions of reader education have evolved. From this we shall examine how the initial expectations changed through

Implications of Students' Use of Libraries

the enquiry into students' habits. We shall go on to examine the information which emerged from this enquiry, and, finally, examine the implications for future faculty/librarian co-operation.

The broad aim of present-day approaches to reader education was stated as far back as 1883 by the President of the University of Columbia :

> A little systematic instruction would start our students in the right methods, that for the rest of their lives all their work in libraries would be more expeditiously accomplished. (p. 46)

Such comments indicate a change in the role of libraries from a custodial to a disseminating one, with an attendant realisation by librarians that active outreach is necessary; that they must engage in some publicity and teaching if patrons are fully to appreciate the richness of collections and to use them with ease despite seemingly complicated procedures and apparently needless regulations. We should also note, in passing, the presumption that the kinds of activity engaged in during studenthood will become part of later lifetime habits.

Dyson (1975) makes a similar point somewhat more forcefully :

> So long as university librarians viewed their primary mission as that of acquirers and organisers of knowledge, such student ignorance (in the use of libraries) was a sad but largely unchanging reality. Now, however, librarians are taking a more aggressive view of their campus role. (p. 9)

Not only must university librarians recognise the need to take positive steps to provide students with the equipment for life-long self-education, but they must also make their own contribution to increasing the cost-efficiency of the university by ensuring that library resources are well-utilised.

The Library Association Record (1949) indicates that by that time a three-stage pattern of reader education has been established and induction into this approach became a formal part of professional training programmes. Carey (1968) suggests that this three-stage pattern remained the norm until at least 1966, and also that this approach was substantially international in its application. The approach was certainly in use in Australian univers-

Implications of Students' Use of Libraries

ities until the early 1970s, and followed this outline :-

> Stage 1 : Introduction to the particular university or college library to be given to all new students ... at the beginning of their first term.
>
> Stage 2 : Introduction to bibliography, both general and with reference to the particular subject, to be given to undergraduates in their first or at the beginning of their second year.
>
> Stage 3 : Advanced instruction in the use of libraries and in bibliographical method, to be given at the beginning of the first year of postgraduate study.
> (Library Association Record, op.cit.)

As the evidence suggests that my own university is not untypical of practice and developments I can use it to show how the above pattern evolved on the ground. Such evidence will also serve to indicate some aspects of professional librarian assumptions and provided the initiative for an enquiry.

To show some appreciation of consumer views we arranged to collect student feedback in a variety of ways. As a result, our initial library orientation tours were modified in three ways. Students - in a similar fashion to that which Billington has earlier recorded - indicated that they were overwhelmed with information during the early days of their first term. Consequently we postponed our tours to occur several weeks after the start of the academic year, introduced fewer services and procedures than had previously been the case, and made the tours open to all students rather than specific to subject groups. It is of some interest to note that recently the tours have been brought forward again as a result of further student complaints at having to wait for library orientation after having started their courses!

The numbers of students attending such tours has remained quite substantial even though many first year courses are based on substantial and detailed reading lists which require very little in the way of detailed knowledge of the working of the

Implications of Students' Use of Libraries

library. Such tours now only concentrate on such basic features as location of texts in the reserve and open collections. They only hint at the hidden treasures which await the users of subject catalogues and bibliographies.

Contact with students on such tours confirmed a general common-sense view that individual students can have very different ideas about what they hope to achieve at university. As Beatty (1977) has suggested, a student's own study contract dictates whether he/she only fulfills the perceived minimum requirements, or chooses to explore further. On this basis, any service designed to meet the academic needs of students, while being based in the first instance on the needs of the instructional system - such as reading lists - and on the demands of the institution providing the service - the library - must also take into account the students' own aspirations and attitudes.

A further complication resides in the aspirations of academic staff for their students. As Beard (1968) discovered in London, there can be tensions between what syllabuses lay down, the actual course presented and what is eventually measured in assessment. An example of a similar and unfortunate discrepancy between librarians, academics and students, from La Trobe, will illustrate that this problem is not peculiar to course design. It will also serve to indicate a widespread problem familiar to all university librarians.

Detailed planning took place to provide library support for a new course on Women in British Society in the Nineteenth Century. Bibliographical skills of a high order seemed called for on two counts: because the course had attracted a large number of women students interested in feminism and eager to trace its roots in many directions; and also because the course required an independent research component for which students were expected to compile their own bibliography. Unfortunately, a departmental requirement, beyond the individual control of the lecturer responsible for the course, was that a major element of assessment should be by examination. This meant that the students felt that they should put more time and effort into preparing for the examination and less into original research for their projects. Their needs for bibliographic skills of a high order were substantially reduced, and the detailed library course provided far too much material which, consequently, they found of little value. A good example, in a library context,

of what Brewer and Hills (1976) have called a
contradiction between the "instructional system"
and the "learning milieu".

Examples such as this are part of the stock in
trade of university librarians, but rarely lead to
radical re-appraisal of professional practices,
either at the level of those solely within the
purview of the library, or at the level of better
library/departmental liaison. Very rarely does one
find evidence of either academics or librarians
openly questioning the assumptions about student
learning which are embedded in their traditional
practices.

The researcher's own reaction to the above
situation was, initially, embedded in her own
assumptions. The answer seemed to lie in acquiring
better information about the academic context of
courses for which reader education was deemed
necessary, together with becoming more aware of the
range of student reactions to their courses. The
kind of reaction which is frequently reported in
professional librarian journals as leading to yet
another library user survey, and, eventually, even
more complex forms of reader induction into library
skills. To provide yet another example of this
traditional response to a traditional problem did
not, on the evidence available, seem a profitable
course of action. A fresh approach appeared to
require two changes from this normal reaction. It
would have to look beyond the question of how
frequently existing services are used in order to
elicit from students their present methods for finding such information as they felt they required -
whether or not those involved library use - as well
as information about student attitudes to libraries
and their courses. In particular, in this latter
area, a new approach would have to examine the ways
in which the two do or should inter-relate. Secondly, the method of enquiry had to allow participants
to determine, to a reasonable extent, the nature of
the information to be collected, the kinds of questions to be asked. Given the concern to find out
about study habits from a student perspective, and
given the view that experience in traditional library practices was no longer sufficient to provide
a basis for such understanding, new ground needed
to be broken.

Attachment to the University of York led to
contacts with the History Department - on the grounds
that at least I would be operating in an academic
area within my specialist competence - and through

Implications of a Students' Use of Libraries

these came opportunities to work closely with staff and students in a specific series of course contexts. New circumstances and new people also prevented the intrusion of assumptions based on past experience. The whole situation provided a basis for the incorporation of "a humanistic appreciation of the complexity and subtlety of the teaching and learning process and the relationship between teacher, student, media, library and environment" (Brewer and Hills, ibid., p. 57) into an enquiry which sought to draw on the strengths of the interpretive tradition.

Initial stages of the enquiry process were based on analysis of data emerging from questionnaires and informal interviews with third year history students at York, and with second year students at the neighbouring University of Bradford - the latter chosen in order to check on assumptions about the universality of findings. Both groups were chosen because of the demands of their courses that they engage in substantial pieces of original research. The piloting, interviewing and final stage questionnaire completion provided what some people have called "progressive focusing" (Brewer and Hills, ibid., p. 62) and others "escalating insights" (Lacey, 1976, p. 61). In other words as new information emerged it was incorporated and the whole approach reviewed in the light of these new factors. This meant that it was always necessary to keep at the forefront of concern the views of staff and students as a suitable corrective to my own interpretations.

The academic perspective on how students would set about information gathering seemed to incorporate the following points - gleaned from a series of informal discussions :-

1. in taught courses the primary source of reading material will be the departmental lists;

2. students will find most reading list items at the library reserve desk;

3. suggestions for further reading will be either requested from tutors or taken from textual references in reading list items;

4. the classified catalogue will be seldom if ever used;

5   if a student wants material on a given
    subject and has no specific initial
    sources, shelf browsing will be the main
    search strategy.

This step by step approach has been presented out of an analysis of a much more extensive description - further details on this and many subsequent points can be found in Newell (1978) - and it is of interest to note that the History Librarian at York offered a similar set of expectations for undergraduate history students.

In addition, though, the History Librarian also offered two further suggestions :-

1   the time of the long essay or solo
    project in the second year is the best
    time to offer reader education to
    history students because it is then that
    they are beginning to work on their own;
    and

2   such reader education is best conducted
    through interviews between the History
    Librarian and each student to discuss
    the individual projects and their likely
    demands.

These two views are clearly consonant with the stages of reader education offered earlier and can, therefore, be taken to indicate the prevalence of this approach. As more information came in from discussions with students it became clear that the official library prescription was of little real value, as it did not make much reference to the actual study habits of the students involved.

Detailed analysis of these later students' responses suggested that the following description would be more relevant :

1   the required overall workload will be
    perceived by students in such a way as
    to prevent much reading beyond official
    reading lists;

2   students will perceive "success" on their
    courses as depending on a mastery of
    information specified by the courses and
    indicated in the official reading lists;

3   the study of history will largely be seen by students as the acquisition of a body of knowledge;

4   the idea of a general orientation to the library in the first year will be approved, but the method employed will be criticised;

5   library staff - either general or subject specific - will be seldom consulted, but if consultation does occur, it will usually be seen as worthwhile by the student;

6   there will be confusion about the role of the subject specialist librarian, despite a widespread feeling that such an appointment is a good idea.

If we compare the picture presented above with those of the earlier sets of assumptions, it is clear that a very different world is being offered for consideration. This new world, the one which, on the students' own admission, is the one they inhabit, determines an approach to the study of history and the practices of information seeking and essay writing which is at odds with the idealised view represented in either the academic or the traditional librarian perspective. In the latter cases the study of history is dependent on original research, and, in principle, relatively unconstrained by the demands of time or assessment. In addition, it is clear that the demands of the assessment requirements of their course figure most significantly in determining all other aspects of a history undergraduate's approach to the subject.

Becker et al (1968) in their Kansas study suggest that students are quick to perceive the "hidden curriculum" and "define" their academic situation in pragmatic terms as one of succeeding by achieving high or inadequate grades," (p. 63-64). By contrast, the academic perspective fitted neatly into the description offered by Entwistle and Percy (1974) in which the student's success lay in "unfolding his personality" in "a liberation from conventional forms of thought", (p. 12). As Becker et al also discovered, such a perspective sees the student pre-occupation with grades as "irrational". According to these other studies, the differences between the attitudes of staff and students lies in the clash between high philosophical aspirations and pragmatic goals. To say this, though, must be to penalise students unduly, since the examinations with which they are concerned, and whose perceived influence has such a determining effect on so much of their academic practices, is the formal tool chosen by the academic staff to test the student's mastery of the course.

Discussion of this apparent conflict with academic staff at both Bradford and York suggests that it is precisely in this area that much ambiguity lies. One academic indicated - and this view had general support amongst all those spoken to - that it would be nice if students read more widely, but that it was the students themselves who wanted and needed a formal prescribed course. "We encourage them to browse a bit, as well as keeping themselves to the reading list suggested. I think the point remains that many students, as they regard their degrees, regard the library as a utilitarian thing." Another academic added the comment that students were "so used to thinking in separate subjects that they were surprised when asked to apply the methodology of their second subject, say economics, to an historical problem." Of these two, in particular, the former offered a short reading list, and the latter a long, annotated one. Both were disappointed in the small amount of outside reading done by their students - and in this their reactions were typical of all academic staff with whom this issue was discussed.

Discussion of the same point with students produced a rather different interpretation. Just keeping pace with the set reading and assignments was a full-time occupation. As one of them put it: "Yes! Working on one's own is encouraged, but I find I just don't have the time." There was a universal "NO" to the question of whether evidence of independent work would make any difference to assessment. The irony of this situation is that both students and staff are dissatisfied, but each assumed that they were operating within unavoidable limitations which the other party had established.

Some of the York students realised that the very act of providing a reading list offered a double message. Certainly the list should be followed as a guide to the seminal works, but with discretion so as to allow time for the additional pursuit of one's own interests. Such students are not only prepared to spend the time on extra reading, but seem perceptive enough to see the choices

Implications of Students' Use of Libraries

implicit in the course structure and are also confident enough to make them. These implicit choices are a major feature of the "hidden curriculum and the student who feels least satisfied with the university is the one who does not realise the existence of these choices but who blindly tries to fulfill all course demands without ever consulting his/her own interests." This description by Beatty (1977, p. 3) suggests a situation analogous to that portrayed by Entwistle and Wilson (1977) in their analysis of student study habits, and also echoes the way in which Edinburgh students play the examination game, which Miller and Parlett (1974) so effectively described.

The matching of our findings with these other results suggests a permanent feature of university learning. Because this is so, it would indicate that expectations on both sides need to be more clearly articulated so that students can become aware of the options available to them, and of the results which follow from the choices they make during their academic careers. It is, however, of critical importance that academic staff recognise that the major responsibility for implementing such changes lies with them. Unless they are prepared to understand that their course structures and syllabuses and assessment demands contain a hidden dimension which can seriously affect the way in which students react to their courses, it is difficult to see how students can be expected to achieve the mature awareness to cope with the implications.

In this context it is interesting to report the way in which Queensland University makes this same point. In a document (Roe and Biggs, 1975) we find "Guidelines for the more efficient use of Library Resources" and this is divided into three categories - for students, library staff and for lecturers. The last guideline for lecturers reads: "If you believe that students should be thrown in the deep-end, and if you believe that most of the foregoing is an unnecessary fuss about matters of trivial importance, please ensure that both your students and the library staff are fully aware that this is what you believe." It is not clear that such approaches have been effective but it is at least a sign that the message is beginning to be understood and communicated.

It is clear from my own findings and those of others that the natural response of students to a complex situation is rational, in that it turns on the individual weighing up of competing demands and

Implications of Students' Use of Libraries

then choosing the most effective course of action to meet the most significant. This can be seen - for example in the context of history staff concern that students stick closely to prescribed reading lists - in terms of the cliche that most students will just do the minumum. Of course, it will always be true that some students are content just to qualify. Such a description is not, however, appropriate for the vast majority of students who were contacted during my enquiries. History students at Bradford and York gave vent to a lot of pent up frustration in discussion. They felt that they were not coping as well as they might with the demands of their courses but, in most cases, lacked two essential skills to help them resolve the problem - a capacity to analyse and understand the overt and covert messages of the learning situation, and the capacity to co-ordinate their responses to their analyses.

The students who made their angry and frustrated comments seemed to lack one of three things which might have enabled them to cope. The first is an attitude as much as a skill, and one without which the others have little value. This is the ability to make decisions and have confidence in one's own judgement. We have already noticed the tiny minority of students who best fulfilled their teachers' expectations were those who read selectively from official reading lists and then chose additional material in their own areas of interest. The transition from relatively dependent secondary school learning to the more independent style which is the hall-mark of the successful university student is likely to be a process rather than an instantaneous change. Because of this it is important that orientation to the work of academic departments needs to include quite explicit statements about the extent and type of independent decision-making and research which is expected. Mere exhortation is not enough, and certainly a single introductory lecture in the first hectic days of the first term will have no real effect. Such statements need to be constantly reinforced during the first year's teaching, in practice, by discussion and through example - and this will require the full co-operation of all the members of an academic department who are involved in such teaching. In addition, a greater degree of open co-operation with librarians, designed to reinforce and encourage these new modes of approach, would also be advantageous. The York students who most apprec-

Implications of Students' Use of Libraries

iated the help given by the History Subject Librarian were those who came to him in desperation because they could not relate to an academic supervisor. One student put it rather despairingly, when describing how she made use of her supervisor, that "I felt he could have done more, but I felt that I should not expect more" - a view which is taken to be indicative of the lack of relationship between tutor and student, and which was quite widespread amongst the students with whom I worked. An alternative view, but with similar implications, was based on the rather sad personal reflection by a student that "needing more help reflects my failure as an historian."

A related skill for which not all students immediately perceive the need is time-management. The usual reason given for failure to read more widely was lack of time. If courses are genuinely over-loaded the cry is obviously real, but more often the problem is as much a failure on the student's part to plan, to set priorities and to estimate realistically the time needed to achieve them. This is yet another reason why bibliographical skills must be part and parcel of university teaching. When a student's anguished cry of "I can't cope!" reaches its most shrill and helpless pitch, it usually means that there are five or six projects all with the same deadline. An awareness of the concurrence of demands, usually emerging from a number of academic staff, and conceivably the more effective planning of assessment work-loads may be part of the answer and should not be overlooked.

However, it is also likely that any amount of course revision will still leave students with problems of peak demand at various times. If the student is to be able to cope sanely and effectively with the management of these peak periods, he/she must -

    know how to find books and journals
    in a library collection
    quickly and easily;
    be experienced enough to be able to estimate
    how much time this is likely to take;
    be skilled enough to know how much work will
    be involved in their effective use;

and, perhaps most importantly,

    must decide at which stages of the competing
    enterprises data collection and analysis
    should begin.

Implications of Students' Use of Libraries

Most students, from my enquiries, seem to operate on the basis of not putting pen to paper until they think they have "all" the necessary information to hand. It also seems to be typical of the student experience that, having operated on this principle, they find, when they begin to write, that much of what they have collected is irrelevant to their argument and they have insufficient time remaining to retrace their steps.

The fact that students operating like this frequently find themselves stuck with a grab-bag of multifarious and disconnected ideas and information out of which they have to cobble a last-minute essay, may be one of the reasons why they often view the library with hostility and disdain. Negative statements from students about libraries are not hard to find. Most of the York students were very disgruntled with the library staff and systems - "One rarely hears anything good about this library" was a common comment - and the Bradford students, though more positively disposed, seldom bothered to make use of the full range of library resources for their projects. The overall effect of all of this is to present something of a "chicken and egg" situation.

In each case, these students showed themselves to have a low level of skill in the use of catalogues and other library systems, as well as a negative attitude to the library as an institution. The constant reinforcement of such an attitude is almost bound to be the consequence of the way in which these students cope with their course demands in the absence of the kinds of skills which offer realistic prospects of survival. In retrospect, it is not surprising to note that the York students simply laughed or snorted when they were asked whether they used the library's classified catalogue. Of those few students who had used this catalogue, those who rated it "useless" tended to be those who read it incorrectly - for example by failing to realise that items like pamphlets are given a special location symbol, and are also placed separately from books with the same classification number.

Students also need to be instructed in the construction of subject headings, because in all three cases where an interviewee claimed there was "Nothing in the classified catalogue" for a particular topic, it turned out that the search had been made under the wrong heading. The two related principles of subject heading - which are, of course,

Implications of Students' Use of Libraries

part and parcel of professional librarianship training - i.e. the concept of a main heading and sub-headings; and the use of a geographical name as main heading, sub-divided by aspect, like 'economic conditions'. Librarians and academics cannot assume that such professional knowledge is automatically acquired by students. The student who, for example, "looked under 'Forests' and could find nothing to help with information about the law of royal forests under Henry the Third", should have gone on to 'Forests: Royal' and would have found, immediately, Hoyt's <u>The Royal Demesne; English Constitutional History, 1066 - 1272</u>.

Such examples are part of the folk-lore of librarians and serve the same purpose as the annual recounting, by academics, of the howlers perpetrated by students in examination papers. In both cases, it can be argued that an alternative interpretation to that offered by the professionals in such circumstances - they demonstrate the ignorance or lack of understanding of the students - is also tenable. The alternative would suggest that students, unless they are specifically directed, cannot reasonably be assumed to pick up the esoteric understanding which is the hall-mark of, and effectively a demonstration of entry into, a narrow professional world.

We must, however, beware of falling into the trap outlined at the beginning of this chapter. The mere exhortation for more reader education services is clearly not a satisfactory response to the needs of students described above. Even the best reader education cannot anticipate every problem. Even academic staff often have recourse to librarians for assistance with their own researches. But in the context of the credibility gap which exists and creates a barrier between students and librarians, and in the context of ways in which students set about coping with their course demands, alternative approaches to the traditional are clearly necessary.

We have already drawn attention to a number of aspects of this troubled relationship between students and librarians, and which only serve to exacerbate the difficulties of effective co-operation, but a further, and equally troubling dimension also needs to be mentioned. Because of their lack of contact, because of their disdainful attitudes, because their lack of expertise makes the library a relatively inhospitable place, many students do not know what kind of assistance they can expect from the library staff. "I don't know what the History Subject Librarian knows," and "Is he there to help one find specific books one knows exist but can't find?" are typical of the comments made to me by students during my enquiry. Students frequently admitted to being fearful of approaching library staff for assistance. "He always looks busy"; "I don't want to seem a fool", are further indications of student responses.

The only sensible course of action would appear to lie in a two-fold change from current practices. Librarians must not be seen as isolated and merely functional and separate from course structures and demands. Academics must recognise the existence of the various dimensions which students face when confronted with their courses and begin to examine ways in which they can minimise the difficulties which course structures create.

The combination of these two will require close working co-operation between academic and librarians in the organisation of study- and library-skills course components. These must not be seen as separate from the actual academic courses but need to be built into the early terms in which attitudes to work and study habits are being formed. The ways in which this can be done will vary from department to department and, conceivably, from university to university according to the variations in the nature of courses and the physical design of institutions.

If it can be done - and nothing significant would appear to stand in the way of its examination - the onus for initiation must rest with academic staff, since theirs is the main responsibility for academic matters. If the library is to retain its significance as a major feature of academic learning and development, then it is critical that students build some rapport with librarians and also with their academic tutors. It is also important that students learn to understand the complementary nature of the skills and advice which academics and librarians can offer. Only through such understanding - and it can only come through practical experience - will students begin to develop the basic competencies which effective utilisation of library resources requires. Only when such competencies have been developed are study habits likely to be modified to enable the majority of students to benefit from the excitement of being able to operate independently within the academic tradition. Students, were such developments to be entertained, would thereby avoid the kinds of frustration experienced by the groups at Bradford and York. These,

Implications of Students' Use of Libraries

as we have seen, because of their misconceptions, fears and lack of skills, deny themselves access to valuable library resources within their own campus confines. Their perceptions of the assessment demands which their courses make, unfortunately contrives to exaggerate rather than minimise these problems.

It would appear that misconceptions, fears, and lack of explicit skills are all too often the stuff out of which the student perspective is woven. To be fair to the student, the misconceptions are not one-sided, and this only serves to make the situation even more complicated. Seldom do university departments and individual academics make clear to their students what is expected of them, and this only serves to aggravate the student search for the underlying system, or "hidden curriculum". To assert, as many academics might, that they do make such things clear in introductory talks to incoming students cannot be sufficient. Billington (Chapter 2) has shown how almost all such well-meaning approaches cancel each other out in the first few days of an undergraduate life. In any case, as we have argued in this chapter, the nature of academic expectations does contain a hidden dimension, and all the clarity of exposition within course outlines and annotated reading lists fails to provide adequate signposting to the nature of the complete academic experience. Only a few students manage to decipher the code for themselves - perhaps these are the potential future academics - but many more could have the hidden message revealed to them through greater concern with the actuality of the learning experience in the early weeks.

The interaction of the consequences of the perceptions of the majority of students with the traditional assumptions with which academic staff appear to operate, conspires to ensure that staff will continue to be disappointed with the frequency with which students decide that the system only requires of them that they get good grades. As Beatty (1977) has argued, and our evidence has confirmed, students who play the superficial system and who never consult - still less, satisfy - their own interests or develop their own study contract are the least satisfied with their university experience.

University librarians, too, will continue to feel some kind of professional resentment that they are only used for trivial enquiries - enquiries which elementary search skills could satisfy - or that they encounter substantial resentment from students when they offer respectable and relevant training courses in library skills. Unless they are provided with an academic context in which they are able to demonstrate, with academic co-operation the relevance of the skills they can offer, they will continue to be perceived, and consequently forced to act as if they are still only custodians and organisers of resources.

While normal practices continue, the university library will have no obvious and natural role for students unless a course is taught in such a way as to oblige him/her to seek out and read certain works. Yet those students who do not read beyond the set texts do themselves a dis-service, because academic staff usually value such intellectual forays, even if they don't request them. Students who indulge in them are also much more satisfied with their courses than those who do not.

Failure to go beyond the narrow confines of course work and prescribed reading lists is not necessarily just a result of a misconception of staff expectations, or of the adoption of study habits the greatest goal of which is to do the minimum. Sometimes it results from an inability to do otherwise; a lack of the skills necessary for independent work. Students who confine themselves to set reading, or choose only courses with set content, frequently lack one of three skills: the ability to make decisions about the direction which their work should take; the ability to set priorities for this work and to estimate how long it will take to complete them; and the ability to use a library to find the information necessary for successful completion of the tasks which they have set themselves.

As other contributors to this book also demonstrate, it is clear that wherever one starts to enquire into aspects of the complex world which represents the student experience, it is the interrelatedness of so many aspects which stands out. The author's concern here was, initially, with more effective reader education programmes to make for more effective use by students of the range of library facilities. From such a limited beginning has grown an understanding which now recognises that to see a library in isolation from the context in which it can most effectively function is grossly to misread the nature of a university. Unless an emphasis is put upon the communality of such an institution of higher education, the prospects of libraries

Implications of Students' Use of Libraries

being seen and used as more than mere book deposits are seriously limited. Unless they can become a central contributor to every student's learning it is difficult to conceive of any peculiar differences which the adjective 'higher' entails in its qualification of this level of education. Without close co-operation between libraries and academics in the planning and conduct of university courses the learning opportunities for the majority of students will continue to be stultified.

Chapter 4

BEING A MATURE STUDENT

(Researched by Elizabeth Rothschild)

The University of York "welcomes applications from 'mature' candidates (that is, those aged 21 or over at the time of application), and a number of such students is admitted each year."(Prospectus, 1983, p.11). An indication of the scale of present numbers of such students has already been given in Table 1.2 Chapter 1 (p.24). Although the researcher for this chapter was not a 'mature' student, within the above definition, she had spent a year out between leaving school and coming to York. It must also be admitted, immediately, that on arrival at University I was convinced that this year's experience had provided me with a wealth of confidence I could not otherwise have gained. I was firmly of the opinion that no-one should be allowed to enter higher education without a year's pause for consideration of life outside the walls of academe.
Although the bulk of this chapter will be concerned to report and analyse an extended and formal enquiry into the experience of mature students at York - and will also, incidentally, draw upon the findings of a series of official investigations conducted by the University's Continuing Education and Teaching Workshop Committees - it is necessary to give a brief account of the inception of this enquiry into activities in which I engaged on my arrival as a new undergraduate at York in 1978. There are two reasons for this. One because it will, by contrast with the later formal approach, provide a salutary reminder of how easy it is to be carried away with one's own ideas of what is normal. The other because, in identifying the continuity of my concerns, I hope to be able to provide evidence to support the interpretations later to be offered.
Such was the extent of my initial commitment to a year's break - shared, I came to discover, by

Being a Mature Student

many other students who had similarly stepped off the educational treadmill for any substantial period - that I immediately embarked on a wholly unguided enquiry amongst all first year students to find out their views about the possibility or experience of such a break. It does not affect the later findings to admit that this initial approach was emotionally rather than analytically organised. That is, both in the preamble, and in a number of the questions asked, my own enthusiasm for a break was apparent.

A number of factors emerged even from this flawed initial approach to sustain my interest and I shall offer them briefly here, both for their own sake and also because a number of them will be taken up when we come to explore the formal enquiry.

My first approach took the form of a postal questionnaire - using the internal mailing system - and although the response was relatively low (only 23% from about 900 students) I was encouraged by the fact that over 200 students had bothered to reply at all to an enquiry from a complete stranger. The questions I used were open-ended and the balance of replies received was weighted in favour of those who had taken some time off before arriving at University - evidence, probably, of the bias built into the questionnaire by my unthinking approach.

Two other respondent biases were also apparent on analysis of the returns: of those who had taken time off, the majority were studying arts or social science courses, and a further majority represented students with private or direct grant school backgrounds - schools where 'Oxbridge' entrance examinations are frequently taken in a seventh sixth form term. For many of these students, the year off had been a natural adjunct to potential Oxbridge entrance, and had been encouraged by both parents and schools. Such schools, too, often offered information about activities worth pursuing in a year away and gave advice on this to their pupils. In the case of the GAP organisation, based at Winchester College, a network of contacts in England and abroad has been created specifically to provide opportunities for travel, voluntary work, experience in industry and so on. For students from these or similar backgrounds, the option of time off before university was realistic and secure; backed up by the financial support of willing and relatively wealthy parents, and given official approval by their schools and teachers. Even when an 'Oxbridge seventh term' was not involved, the activities undertaken - travel, secretarial courses, voluntary work

- suggested that the student was receiving, in varying degrees, some economic help from parents, and also benefiting, probably, from the same network of connections established by their school.

Such factors contrasted with the replies from the minority, who had not taken time off. The majority of these seemed to have only the vaguest understanding of its existence as a possibility, and were equally often unaware of the opportunity to apply for deferred entry to a university. It appeared that only a few universities openly encourage this in their prospectuses. However, since York is one which does, I interpreted these results as indicating that it was up to schools both to provide information about such possibilities and also to provide support and encouragement to their pupils to take such action.

Even the few respondents who had considered the possibility often found it hard to obtain information on organisations to contact and found their teachers actively discouraging. Students mentioned that their schools had emphasised the need to keep up the momentum of studying, and seemed to imply a loss of motivation and ability to anyone contemplating not proceeding directly to university if a place was available. Such students also reported that their parents reflected similar attitudes, emphasising also the need to qualify as soon as possible in order to improve job prospects in an increasingly gloomy climate. Those who had still considered the option of time out against all these pressures, and in the further knowledge in almost every case that there would be no financial help for them in such a venture, took their own look at the rising unemployment figures and themselves decided not to risk spending a year on the dole. A few had no choice at all because of the presence of older siblings in education and this created a further financial pressure militating against personal freedom of action.

The pressure perceived by science students from all backgrounds appeared very strong, and most had come straight to university. They were predominantly concerned about possibly losing a grasp on the vast amount of actual information they felt their courses of study to require, and were most concerned to avoid any interruption of their studies. Some of these students also mentioned the need for further, post-graduate training and the consequent extension of study before entering employment.

The arts students who replied, and especially

those who had taken time off, argued that such experience would enhance their studies. Critically, though, these views tended to reflect some kind of class bias in that many of the replies talked about "getting to know working class people for the first time", or "understanding what manual jobs were really like", or "appreciating the privilege of higher education for the first time". It is clear that such views will only reflect attitudes of a proportion of university students, and the opportunities which a year out could provide would be unlikely to offer much prospect of analogous opportunities to students from working class backgrounds. Paradoxically, it is most likely that the broadening of experience and a widening of class contacts for many students will only arise through university opportunities. This was one of the first results to emerge which began to shake my initial certainty of the universal value of a break between school and higher education.

Another conclusion which I drew from this preliminary approach, also led to further revision of my own views without diminishing my commitment to further research. This was that whether students made a break in their education or did not do so seemed in no sense to be an active decision. Both groups appeared to do what the majority of their school peers did when heading for higher education. Both groups, too, seemed to be subjects of substantial pressure at home and at school and their eventual decisions were consistent with the pressures to which they admitted being subject. Another factor emerged in a number of replies which further supported this image of a predominant peer group approach to this decision. Those not taking time off, and not having contact with many who did, mentioned fears of being "too old" had they taken time off. Those taking time off had many contemporaries doing the same, and therefore expected to encounter others, and mentioned no considerations of this kind.

One further small group of respondents served both to make me question my initial assumptions even further, and also to indicate to me that my own experience was not necessarily typical of all 'mature' students. These were the students who had taken many years off, and in many cases my respondents indicated that the initial break from school was not initially seen as the start of a period which would, inexorably, lead eventually to entry into higher education. In most cases higher education had been very far from any ideas they held at that time. These students, although they were very few in number who replied to my questionnaire, also served to indicate to me that by not subjecting my own views to critical reflections before embarking on my enquiry, I had, in fact, produced a questionnaire to which they found it difficult to reply. Many of my questions left no opportunity, in spite of their relative open-endedness, for them to offer their own substantial experiences. Their concerns, it appeared, were more involved with the process of deciding to come to university than with describing their experiences in the 'outside world'.

A few quotations will serve to illustrate the difference in approach of these students. Coming to York became "a conscious decision and application on my part." Another wrote: "Rather than wondering whether or not I would be able to live up to the standards imposed by the university, I began to think in terms of what I could get out of the experience." Another comment also seemed significant: "Had I taken the advice of my headmaster and stayed on at school and then gone straight to university, I would have been permanently damaged by my attitude to my work." These students, it seemed to me, were not at the University as a matter of course - as were almost all my acquaintances, whether we had taken time out or not - or for want of anything better to do. The decision to come had often been a difficult one, was certainly protracted, and often required substantial re-organisation of permanent family commitments.

In addition to this early questionnaire I also sent one to academic staff designed to explore what differences, if any, they could observe in students who had taken time off. Again there was a very limited response - perhaps not surprising in the circumstances - but there were also pointers in the replies received which echoed some of my student reactions. Science staff, for example, argued that any interruption in studies could only disrupt a student's academic career - thus providing a basis of support for student expectations. Staff in the arts and social sciences suggested that any reactions would depend on personalities, but that there were noticeable differences in confidence in seminars in the early stages of a course. No differences were noted in terms of settling down to academic work, nor in the quality of work produced. The most significant differences noted in staff replies concerned students who had come to university after a break of several years. While these students were not necessarily at the top of the academic spectrum, their work was always felt to be very good, and their contributions to seminars and tutorials improved these enormously. As one lecturer commented: "I see no value in the year off as a lark, or as an exercise in growing up, but the really mature students are invaluable."

The overall results of my early enquiries thus took many forms. I realised that any further enquiry would need to be more carefully conceived and executed; that a whole series of new issues beyond my original understanding had emerged; and that some of my initial cherished assumptions had become at best questionable. Most important, it seemed that there were two clearly identifiable groups of mature students - those taking a brief break between school and university, and those making a significant life and career change a long time after leaving school.

A year off was highly valued by those who had experienced it, but the other group saw the situation very differently. In both cases the consequences of the break seemed more to affect the social and personal dimensions of their life than enhance their capacity to benefit academically. Both groups appeared to settle in easily and quickly and with few of the problems which Billington (see Ch.2) has suggested are the lot of students coming straight from school. These mature students also appeared to socialise more with others of similar background - again a feature which appears to be common to a number of student sub-groups. It clearly required further work to examine the question of whether mature students coped better with the complicated and often conflicting demands of university life. Social ease and confidence - which was universally reported in my initial survey but is not necessarily attributable to a year away - is not a necessary adjunct to academic success.

Mention has already been made of a number of official University enquiries into aspects of mature students' experience. Both because these give some indication of the academic perspective, as well as because of the detail they provide on a number of questions, we shall use these findings as a basis for the eventual discussion of my own, later enquiry. It should be noted here, though, that I did not have access to the official findings until my own, later enquiries had been completed.

There were two kinds of official enquiry

Being a Mature Student

mounted through various University committees. One was a questionnaire sent to 150 mature undergraduates out of the 275 such students present in the academic year 1981/82. All 90 students aged 25 or more on entry were contacted, and the remaining 60 were chosen at random from the younger mature students. The other academic approach required departmental responses to comments made from a Teaching Workshop seminar on 'Learning and the Mature Student'. We shall deal with aspects of these in turn.

Replies to the student questionnaire were received from 49 students, distributed as Table 1 below indicates. It should be noted that the figures show that the replies were heavily weighted towards the older mature students - this adding a further limitation to that already provided by the limited response rate. Table 2 below gives the subject balance of the respondents and indicates that no further bias emerged from this factor.

Table 4.1 Age Profile of Responding Mature Students

	Age				
	21/25	26/30	31/40	41/50	51+
Respondents as % of all respondents (N=49)	22.45	42.86	24.49	8.16	2.04
Mature undergraduates as % of all mature u/gs (275)	67.27	18.18	10.91	2.55	1.09

Table 4.2 Subject Balance of Respondents

	Main Subject		
	Arts	Social Sciences	Sciences
Respondents as % of all respondents (N=49)	36.73	51.02	12.25
Mature undergraduates as % of all mature u/gs (275)	36.00	50.67	13.37

Where quotations are given in the following analysis they are taken (with permission) from the official report on the findings of the enquiry. The report itself had two main sections: one dealing

Being a Mature Student

with learning, the other with living as a mature student. We shall follow this division here, except that it is worth starting with a comment from the 'living' section. In this, attention is drawn to comments from a number of replies to the effect that the definition of 'mature' needs some examination. The official University distinction of 21+ "means that the differences between the older and youngest mature students are wider than with mature/non-mature students at the bottom end of the scale." Views of older students on this matter were also echoed by those in the 21 - 25 age range, "who stated that they felt there was little difference between their experience as students and that of undergraduates younger than themselves."

We shall return to this point later, but it serves here as a context against which a number of comments from the 'learning' section of the report can be set. In many of the comments reported in this section there is an indication of comparisons being made either with current 18 year olds, or else by the mature students with their views of themselves as they had been at 18.

Learning styles figured largely in many of these comments, as well as aspects of producing formal work and assessment procedures. Responses quoted ranged from "I find mature students more interested in 'learning', others seem more interested in gaining a degree", through "Younger students can read and write faster, therefore in most cases learn quicker; they can lack stamina however", and "The difference (i.e. between mature and non-mature undergraduates) probably lessens as time goes on and other students gain confidence" to "I recognise the need to pace myself and work consistently rather than sporadically as I suspect I would have been tempted to do at 18."

A major emphasis in this section of the report, though, recognises "the stronger motivation of the mature student". The report opens, in fact, with the general comment "that the strength of motivation felt by most mature students reconciles them to the difficulties they clearly encounter over learning techniques."

Integration into the academic life of a department was the other main issue explored in the report. On this matter it was noted that "there was little uniformity in the replies; as several respondents pointed out, such a capacity is a function of personality, not age." The connection was noticeable, however, in terms of the effect of social life on academic integration - a factor which appears to be common to all the chapters reporting student experience, and one which has major implications for the restructuring of academic life. Again there was variation in response, ranging from "I find that there is a different relationship between staff and myself than between staff and school-leavers", through "I feel personally that tutors/school-leavers still find it difficult to get over a classroom-type relationship. As a mature student I feel in between this and find it difficult to handle", to the saddest and most extreme response: "the isolation felt by mature students of older years has to be experienced to be believed. Often participation in seminars is the only conversation I have during the day."

This part of the official report concluded with a series of suggestions - to which more detailed reference will be made in Chapter 7 - about measures to meet the special learning requirements of mature students. The point to emphasise, though, is the preface to these suggestions, which notes that "the specific measures suggested would mostly be of advantage not just to mature students but to all students irrespective of age."

The 'living' section of the report opens with a comment which suggests that the initial situation of mature students has close parallel with that of ordinary students: in terms of adapting from a highly structured life to that of an undergraduate with a lot of spare time to organise and use. However, such feelings appeared to evaporate relatively quickly for most students. What was noticeable, though, was that the contacts, for any mature student, tended predominantly to be with other mature students - although not all agreed with this. The majority view is best expressed in the following response:

> In generalising about what I feel and what I know other mature students feel, it is almost impossible to socialise with people who have just left school and/or have no work experience. Mature students tend to stick together, and form the basis of their social lives round groupings away from the University and/or continue with their 'pre-University social lives'.

Such a view is taken to reflect clearly the distinction, already noted, between the 25+ older

Being a Mature Student

mature student and the younger group who are much nearer in age and experiences to the students coming straight from school. A further sub-division of this distinction is made by considering the small group of mature students who are married - with or without children. For such students it was noted that family commitments tend to provide an alternative social base to that of the University and, in any case, will produce commitments which reduce the time for University contacts. Having children adds further to these pressures and frequently ensures that the only concern for the University is in terms of work commitments - a situation very different from that of the ordinary student. A number of mature students with such commitments did, however, indicate that they had turned this apparent disadvantage to their own benefit "not least (by being able to) 'escape' from the campus and its strange disjointedness from the city."

The report drew attention to an element of uncertainty in the response as to whether or not mature students should be singled out for any kind of special attention. Answers seemed to oscillate between suggesting that mature students did have particular problems and indicating that a 'low profile' approach was preferable. Yet others indicated that even if there were special problems, mature students, like all students, would simply have to cope with whatever problems occurred. Here, mention was sometimes made of the special sense of commitment which it was felt that mature students possessed.

It is worth noting, finally, that the report concluded by stressing advantages to be set against any problems which might have emerged from the enquiry. Central to this conclusion was the strong feeling that mature students should not isolate themselves or be isolated; that they had many things to offer and much to gain from complete integration and involvement with all other members of the University community. It was, however, pointed out that such comments sat ill with earlier ones which indicated a fair degree of isolation, and provoked the question of whether, in the circumstances which had been described, "the University and younger undergraduates absorb the benefits mature students offer by osmosis?"

In another paper, which emerged from the University Committee on Continuing Education and was also concerned with mature students, reference was made to the conclusions of the earlier Teaching

Workshop seminar on this topic. The quotation, given below, acts as a useful summary of some of the main findings which have emerged so far:

> In general it seemed that the social difficulties encounted by mature undergraduates were perhaps greater than might be thought, whereas the learning difficulties varied from student to student and were not in any event inherently different from those encountered by younger undergraduates.

Departmental responses to the circulation of such information and discussion papers contained a variety of views - generally reflecting differences in departmental experience with mature students. Departments were concerned with what they perceived as the different strategies of learning adopted by mature students, others thought that not enough was done to share information, felt to exist on the campus, about ways of helping with particular problems. Some thought that concentration on mature students had helped to bring to notice a range of problems common to all students and that the adoption of general approaches would be universally helpful. In these latter cases, concern was frequently expressed that departments should reflect more carefully on the expectations they made of students and explore ways - e.g. more deliberate training in essay writing, clearer indications of what makes an essay acceptable, production of documents outlining approaches to successful learning - of providing assistance. Yet other replies commented on the value of really mature students being able to call on their extra-university experience, but contrasted that, in some cases, with the difficulties they found in coping with the abstract or conceptual side of a discipline. Where mature students had undertaken some kind of preparatory study before coming to university, this was felt to be helpful in adapting to academic routines of work.

It is against this background of official reactions to mature students' self-reflection and departmental perceptions of their own experiences with mature students, that we can now proceed with the issues which emerged from the later enquiry conducted by the author following the interesting, but ill-conceived trial venture. This second approach was based on a commitment to an interpretive model of enquiry and both formal and informal contacts were used to provide opportunities for ex-

Being a Mature Student

tensive discussion, of a predominantly free-wheeling kind, on any issues connected with university experience. Formal approaches lead, usually, to discussions taking place in the student's own room - which was taken as an aid to confidence and openness of response - and were based on a random sample, controlled for subject and gender, of first year students. It appeared that intensive time-tabling created a bias in favour of arts and social science students, but given the earlier evidence of the preponderance of a break among such students the lack of substantial comment from science students is not seen as a major hindrance.

A number of other points also distinguished between arts and science students whether or not they had taken time out. Three of them are of significance here: vocational orientation, timetabling and socialising.

Most of the science students already had a clear vocational aim and saw their period at university as a stage in achieving their goals. A point made time and time again concerned the advice given to them at home and at school to the effect that a break in their education would be disadvantageous on two counts: in terms of delaying entry into later occupation or later post-graduate training, and in terms of losing a conceptual grasp of their subject. The few science students who had even contemplated a break in their education had considered looking for work experience related to their eventual occupational interests but had not followed this through after finding difficulty in gaining such experience without more advanced qualifications.

Arts students showed much less clear vocational intentions and, if they did make a break, found a very wide range of jobs, and seemed little concerned that these had any connection with postgraduate employment. Only two of these students expressed a clear statement of vocational aims and had deliberately looked for and found related work. A man had done a year's social work, and a woman worked in a bookshop, intending, after graduation, to enter publishing.

These differences apart, it is fair to summarise these views as indicating that those without time off regarded university as a means to an end or the logical continuation of their education which they had never seriously questioned. Those who took time off saw it more as an end in itself and valued the opportunities that university provided to study and to enjoy the variety of social experience available.

The work patterns of students also showed a clear distinction between arts and science students. Arts students were generally eased into their course with introductory terms or courses and also had much more time free of formal academic commitments. For them the perceived contrast with school was considerable and both allowed and appeared to reinforce a view of university life in which socialising played a major role. Arts students who had come straight from school admitted to being bewildered by a perceived lack of guidance and felt overawed by mature students, saying that they seemed better read and more articulate. Those who had taken time off admitted to some nervousness at the prospect of beginning academic work, but had soon readjusted and further enjoyed the freedom of organising their own study. They enjoyed the variety of opportunities for meeting new people, but felt less enthralled by the frenetic socialising of the first few weeks of term.

Students without time off often commented on how much more socially adept the mature students seemed and, therefore, how difficult it would be to make relationships with them. A number of these students also admitted to being exhausted with deliberate attempts to meet as many new people as possible in the first few weeks of term, and then to being upset when such openness significantly reduced. Many of them also admitted that what had appeared to be the 'fun' of the start of term had, in fact, been a lonely and nerve-wracking time for them - thus reinforcing the points which Billington has mentioned in Chapter 2. Those with time off, by contrast indicated that they had paid little attention to this organised initiation period, had only joined a few societies in which they were particularly interested, and had only attended meetings which they felt would be of real value.

Science students, by contrast, had started with full timetables which, like their sixth form school experience, effectively structured their lives. Their patterns of work appeared to be constant throughout the term. Their friendships tended to be within two main groups - either from students along the corridors of the college where they lived, or else from their own subject year groups. They tended to belong to fewer societies - most joining their subject society and a sports club. With these extra-curricular attachments they felt they had little time for anything but their subject time-

tables and the work they were expected to complete.
It is of interest to note that more science than arts students mentioned the campus when discussing their choice of university. The advantage of campus residence was keenly felt, specifically in relation to the need to attend early lectures daily, and they expressed little interest in the range of alternative experiences which the neighbouring city could offer. Arts students, on the other hand, placed more emphasis on the prospects of off-campus residence, certainly expressed interest in the city and spent much time exploring it. Students with time off were almost universally in favour of the prospect of eventual off-campus living, seeing independence and distance as significant advantages.

A further difference with the mature students emerged as many other undergraduates mentioned the frequency with which they went home at weekends during this first term and also indicated that they had more visitors from home than did mature students. This seemed to indicate a difference in terms of relative independence between the two groups - a factor substantially reinforced by the few mature students with families in the city. These - as has already become apparent from the earlier studies - need to be clearly distinguished from other categories of mature students.

The time off experiences of those who had made only a limited break between school and university were varied. A number had gone abroad both for work and travel, others had taken skill-based courses - particularly of the secretarial variety - while the remainder had been involved in various kinds of occupations, mainly manual, office or in the retail trades. Only one person admitted to having read a lot during the break, while almost everyone else mentioned a deliberate intention to eschew all intellectual pursuits during the period.

Apart from one student - who had taken time off against the wishes of her parents, and who had admitted to difficulties in settling down to work - all the other students felt they had gained enormously from the experiences of the break. Where such benefits did not accrue directly to their academic work, the personal reaction was felt to complement any academic disadvantages. Frequently mentioned were the evidence of proving one's capacity to live independently and be fully responsible for one's life. In addition, a point emerging from the first enquiry also surfaced here. This concerned the class distinction in some responses to the break as a means of broadening a person's contacts with other people. As was noted earlier, the social mixing experienced by many from privileged backgrounds during their break occurred for many others on coming to university. The self-confidence which the mature students often admitted to during these interviews was frequently supported by my own impressions. The mature students were more open, answered questions more readily, were prepared to argue and consider their views to a much greater extent than those interviewees who had come straight from school. Mature students also often used the interview as a vehicle to satisfy their own needs - by asking for information about the University, courses, staff, or by enquiring about off-campus accommodation. Where the other students asked any questions at all, these were almost always about what was necessary to survive the university experience.

To see the extent to which any of these differences were maintained as the students became more accustomed to being at university, follow-up interviews were conducted much later during the same first year - mainly towards the end of the second term. These interviews were much longer than the earlier ones and much more discursive, in that many more students were now prepared to take control and dictate the lines of development.

Again, it is possible to see differences between arts and science students - though not the same as the ones previously noted - but it was also possible to see that some notable differences between mature and other students at the initial interviews had substantially narrowed.

One new source of difference for arts students resulted from the fact that they had begun to have academic work assessed and receive feedback from staff about their performances - something which had happened to science students from the beginning. In many cases, therefore, arts students were now beginning to express doubts about their subject or about their ability to cope. Where this occurred with science students it was in the first set of interviews. By the second series, they had usually resolved any initial problems they had experienced.

The arts students expressing doubts about their subject were those who had taken time off, whilst those wondering about their ability to cope had come to university straight from school. The break appeared to have provided a basis for early analysis

of difficulties and a capacity to organise one's
time - things which the other students had to learn
after arrival. It is at least conceivable, therefore, that this earlier engagement with the full
demands of courses was the source of the doubts
expressed about the nature of the course being
followed. However, it is also possible that the
extra-campus experience had also provided a source
for more significant questioning about the purpose
of higher education in individual cases. Unfortunately there were not enough responses to allow this
to be explored.

A word which occurred frequently in the arts
interviews was 'claustrophobia'. Most of them were
suffering from this in greater or lesser degree.
One described the change vividly as "the holiday
camp becoming a prison camp." Those with time off
seemed to be coping with this marginally better,
usually because they appeared to be less tied to
the campus either physically or mentally: they
seemed less dependent on campus sources for interest
or support. Generally speaking, therefore, by the
end of their second term, arts students were finding
their university life harder and, at times, depressing - something which none of them had anticipated.
Mature students seemed better able to cope, but all,
in spite of difficulties, seemed more confident and
at ease than on the occasion of the earlier interviews.

The situation of the science students was
little different from what they described at the
first interviews. Some found campus life a little
irritating, but the majority still extolled its
convenience in relation to the still substantial
work demands of their courses. Very few of these
students used the self-catering facilities available to them and again the time factor - constant
feature of their university experience - was mentioned as the main barrier to such activity. A
number of wry comments were made by these students
about how much quieter their residential blocks were
now that arts students, too, had begun to work. A
number also offered comments about how their new
perceptions of their own abilities were different
from those with which they had arrived. In some
cases this had already led to a major readjustment
of eventual occupational interests.

By the end of that first year, through informal
contacts, it was possible to add a further gloss on
these interviews. The situation for arts students
had improved: their equilibrium seemed to have been

restored: they seemed to have a clearer perception of the nature of all aspects of university life and were able to balance these effectively. It was, however, impossible to distinguish between mature and other students in terms of confidence and social ease.
 Contrasting the conclusions I would now draw with those assumptions which characterised my initial enquiries a number of major issues can be examined. The distinction between the really mature student and those merely taking a break of usually at most one year between school and university seems of critical importance to any further understanding. The substantial difference between the total university experience of arts and science students is another feature to emerge with greater complexity than I would have believed. The view that leaving a university before completing a course should be construed as failure is also one with which I would now profoundly disagree. I shall conclude this chapter with some reflections on these issues in the light of the various kinds of information on mature students which have been presented.
 While there are clearly substantial initial differences in the ease with which mature and non-mature students adapt to university life, such differences appear to be temporary. By the end of the first year there were no discernible differences either in coping with social life or in coping with the academic demands of courses. Success at university does not, therefore, seem to be significantly associated with a break in education. The exception here must always be those mature students who have, on the whole, made some mid-career change of direction in which attendance at a university plays a major part. For these students there is very little sign that they ever become full members of the university community in the way that the majority of other students do, whether mature or not.
 Within the life of the university one other difference could be noticed and which did not emerge from any of the enquiries reported here. Examination of the students who took positions of responsibility within the Union, other societies or at the college level, shows a noticeably clear distinction. At the University level the vast majority of students in official positions over a number of years came from those who had made a break in their education before arriving at York. College posts - and the Introduction has made clear the existence of this separate level of organistion at York - seemd to be

seemed to be the preserve of students coming straight from school. Two interpretations seem to be possible here. One of these would suggest that the social ease and confidence which mature students express, and are perceived by others to possess, allows them to be more readily considered as credible contenders in student elections. This, coupled with the worldly experience which such students will have acquired through their time off, may make it more likely that they, themselves, will also see such student positions as being attractive. If this is the case it is likely that similar features will be seen at all universities and, perhaps even more significantly, at the national NUS level.

The other interpretation will take account of the existence of this special, college-based tier of organisation at a university like York. The existence of student positions of many kinds at this alternative level, will certainly provide the possibility of administrative and official experience to other students who become mature through their time at university. In universities which do not have an alternative level of authority such students will be at a natural disadvantage in coming later to the notice of their peers as compared with the mature students who will have settled in more rapidly.

One of the major difficulties for any student coming to university is balancing their social and academic life. The overwhelming nature of the variety which is opened to them immediately on arrival came through my own enquiries and supplemented the detail which Billington has already given. For mature students the problems of adaptation are different from those experienced by the non-mature student. The mature student seems to be able to make appropriate choices relatively quickly and so concentrate efforts and energies into a restricted range of activities. The non-mature student is more likely to waste a great deal of time in taking on too many commitments in the initial stages, and takes some time to find out, from this large array, which ones are most of interest. By contrast, the non-mature students adapt more readily to work and experience fewer qualms, initially, about academic expectations. Mature students may be better, in the early stages, at organising their time to meet the academic demands made of them, but they feel greater problems will be encountered through having made a gap in their education. Paradoxically, the impression given by mature students, especially in arts courses with a premium on small-group teaching, is that they encounter few academic difficulties because they seem prepared to offer contributions while their non-mature peers stay silent. Again, though, it must be noted that by the end of the first year such differences appear to have been resolved. For science students, the intensive time-tabling they experience at university reinforces their views that any break in their formal education would be significantly counter-productive.

Many of the problems which students encounter at university are connected with doubts about their choice of subject, choice of institution, or even with the decision to come to university at all. These problems seem to occur for all students at some time or another, but they are extreme for more students than many people seem to credit. The really mature students, for example, become very concerned if they experience a very bad period of academic difficulties. In such situations they become very concerned about the major decision to change their lives which being at university usually entails for them. However, the evidence would suggest that such students, though very few in number, are both personally resilient and also are able to use their extra-university social situations as therapy.

For science students, on the other hand, the continuity of time-filled academic life between school and university, coupled with the evidence they give of having formed occupational aims very early, appears to prevent the emergence of many critical identity problems. The only evidence which emerged was a scaling down of occupational aspirations to fit more readily with a reappraisal of abilities early in the university experience. The similarity of views between the advice reported by these students from their teachers with those of academic staff on the advisability of a break for science students would indicate that there is likely to be little success in any moves to try to encourage breaks for all students. At the same time the existence of such an overlap of views does raise the question of the benefits to industry of receiving annual intakes of new, graduate, recruits with no experience, from the age of 5, outside the world of formal education.

It is the students who come straight from school who are likely to face the most serious problems in respect of identity crises, since the overwhelming evidence reported here suggests that the University is where many of them begin to appreciate the detailed nature of their own personalities and interests. The inter-relationship between confidence and a capacity to cope with competing and complex demands is one feature of these enquiries which has been borne in on me. Consequently, I am led to surmise that many non-mature students remain at university and fail to fulfill their potential, and there seem to be two factors which reinforce these unfortunate decisions. One of these lies in the stigma which appears to be associated with any decision to leave a university course before completion. This is something which a number of students mentioned in the course of describing their own feelings that after experiencing the University they did not feel ready to reap the benefits that were available to them. They were worried about the reactions of their friends, their parents, their tutors, their previous schools and prospective employers. Whether these feelings were justified is beside the point; what is important is that these students believed they would be permanently labelled as failures if they followed the dictates of their reasoning and broke off their studies.

This is not to say that many students were found to be in deep despair, nor that they were battling on against insuperable pressures and heading for breakdown. What did emerge was that many students would have welcomed an opportunity to drop out of their present university courses for a substantial period - even, in some cases, insisting that they felt, at the time, they might never resume their studies in this kind of institution. It must also be admitted that York, as a small campus university, probably provides greater opportunities for students to talk over problems like these with academic supervisors than larger, more dispersed universities can arrange. From the student point of view, though, it must be stressed that admitting such ideas to a tutor was felt to be tantamount to admitting to an incapacity to cope - and such was not the case.

It must always be pointed out that York, with its high level of entry qualifications and all its courses at the same, honours, level, does allow for ease of transfer of students between courses although, officially, it discourages students from applying for one course with a view to changing on arrival. There is, however, much evidence of transfer taking place as between single and combined subject degrees at York and these opportunities clearly help many students to achieve a suitable academic niche as a result of changes in interests after arrival. This still leaves what might be a large group of students, who give every outward appearance of being able to cope with their courses, but who would really wish to defer the experiences until a substantially later stage of life. The mechanics of grant aid, coupled with already noted perception of stigma, mean that many students eventually graduate and leave the University incompletely satisfied with their three years' experience. Whether the American system of course credits is the answer to this may be taken up in later chapters, but it seems clear that if the government is concerned with value for money from state investment in higher education, recognition of this problem, and a detailed enquiry to determine its extent, should become priorities for action. The Open University has already shown that the traditional three year undergraduate programme, taken consecutively with schooling, and requiring high-level A level grades for entry, is not the only way to provide graduate qualifications. The University of Buckingham has also shown that the three term year, with long vacations, is not sacrosanct when considering the design of undergraduate programmes.

In reading a variety of books and articles I examined a number of works which discussed the difficulties students faced at university and the effects on their academic performance. Although most academic writers had advanced their thinking beyond the position that any student who left was simply a failure, few had taken their analyses beyond consideration of factors such as class, sex, I.Q., and personality ratings. While there are undoubtedly significant correlations to be explored between some of these factors and academic progress, what also needs to be examined is the whole educational process which prepares an 'able' student for a future in university. Leaving university might even be considered to be a success in many cases, but before encouragement is given to enlarging opportunities for easier withdrawal from courses it will also be necessary to ensure that adequate provision is made for return to full-time education.

It was the apparent lack of perception of opportunities available to them - both inside the University and outside in the real world - which mature students frequently described as their view of the attitudes of the non-mature student. Mature students found it infuriating to see how younger students 'wasted' their opportunities in ignorance of how unique their situation was.

Thus, while my own views of the immeasurable benefits of breaking the continuity of education between school and university have been substantially modified. I still hold to the view that the decision to come to university should be more consciously and directly made. It is clear that this is so for the really mature student. It is less clear that it is the case for students coming directly from school or even for those who make a break of a year between school and university. In both these cases the evidence suggests that the decision to come to university is unthinking, an assumption that has been a part of their lives for a number of years before any UCCA forms are ever completed. To this end, I am forced to the paradoxical conclusion that the easiest way to encourage this is to alter the nature of entrance requirements in order to reduce the ease with which the almost mechanical acquisition by eighteen year olds of appropriate A level grades becomes an almost automatic right of entry to an experience from which many will not really benefit.

A consequence of such a change - after the initial problems of coping with a likely inrush of people who would like to try the university experience but who would not normally meet the traditional entry requirements - would be an increase of substantial proportions in the numbers of mature students making conscious decisions in the light of detailed reflection on other experience. Since it seems, on the evidence of the official enquiries reported here, that academic staff are beginning to take the problems of student learning seriously through an initial concern with a perception of the peculiar difficulties of mature students, there will be the additional benefit that teaching, as well as research, could become a major area of interest for all academic staff. The results of such a change would then be far-reaching for all students.

Chapter 5

BEING AN OVERSEAS STUDENT

(Researched by Barbara Gillie)

In December 1982 Lord Scarman delivered, in the House of Lords, a critical judgement which upset a series of assumptions about definitions of being an overseas student, (2 W.L.R., 16, 1983). In the light of this judgement the government was left with two options: to leave the situation as the House of Lords' decision had made it, thereby substantially expanding the numbers of potential students qualifying for mandatory grant support; or to amend the appropriate legislation and guidelines in order to ensure that their original intentions, overthrown by the House of Lords' decision, were manifest. At the time of writing, whilst the Secretary of State has announced his intentions to modify the appropriate regulations, no new guidelines are available either to grant awarding bodies or to universities considering which scale of fees to charge to students.
One consequence of this is that at present universities de facto will continue to operate in terms of the guidelines first established by the UGC in 1967. In these, to quote from the example of the document which the University of York sends to prospective students, "Classification for the purpose of student grants is not the same as for applications and fees". Critical to the confusion which thus still remains in connection with the definition of an overseas student is the point upon which Lord Scarman's judgement turned - "the meaning to be given in the context of the Education Acts to the words "ordinarily resident in the United Kingdom"" (W.L.R., op.cit.), and the apparently similar phrase in the UGC guidelines that "An overseas student is one whose normal place of residence is outside the United Kingdom."
It must always be a dangerous practice to para-

phrase a legal judgement or to take quotations from a lengthy judgement without detailing the context. However, it is worth noting that Lord Scarman indicated the nature of the legal distinction between the two terms 'ordinarily resident' and 'normal place of residence'. The former "refers to a man's abode in a particular place or country which he has adopted voluntarily and for settled purposes as part of the regular order of his life for the time being, whether of short or long duration," (ibid. p.26 H). The latter term would seem to imply the use of the alternative legal definition of a 'real home' or 'domicile' the determination of which is "dependent upon a refined, subtle, and frequently very expensive judicial investigation of the devious twists and turns of the mind of man," (ibid. p.28 E). On the difference, Lord Scarman commented: "By giving the words (ordinarily resident) their natural and ordinary meaning one helps to prevent the growth and multiplication of refined and subtle distinctions in the law's use of common English words. Nothing is more confusing and more likely to bring the statute law into disrepute than a proliferation by judicial interpretation of special meanings, when Parliament has not expressly enacted any," (ibid. p.28 H).

Given the effects of the government's decision, announced in Parliament on 1 November 1979, that "as from the start of the academic year 1980/81, all overseas students who begin courses of higher and further education in Great Britain would be expected to pay a fee covering the full cost of tuition", (D.E.S. 1980, para 2.35), the nature of the House of Lords' decision has substantial financial consequences for students and for universities and LEAs. However, it should be noted that simplicity of the division between home and overseas students was further modified by announcements on 1 April 1980 and 9 September 1980 respectively, that "European Community students would pay the home rate of tuition fee from 1 September 1980 onwards", and "that refugees within the meaning of the United Nations Convention would be treated as home students for both fee and award purposes," (D.E.S. 1982, para 3.39).

We make no apologies for opening this chapter with the above account of some recent developments relating to the official and statutory definitions of who counts as an overseas student. Such developments have had many effects, and universities have responded in various ways to the consequent reductions in the numbers of overseas students prepared and able to support full cost fees and subsistence requirements. The recent initiation of a scholarship fund, and the alteration of the status of students from Hong Kong, suggest that the many complaints from universities and foreign governments have had some effect. Our concern here, though, is not to enter the political debate about differential fees, nor the many other debates about issues connected with the benefits - short-term to university communities, and long-term to future attitudes to Britain - of continuing a policy of open access, on an international basis, to British universities. Our purpose is, instead, to direct attention to the confusion which surrounds the nature and status of an overseas student entering a British university.

While the findings of the enquiry into overseas student perceptions, which forms the basis for the remainder of this chapter, will also deal with other aspects of this confusion, it is as well to be reminded that any confusion within a particular university has a wider legislative context. It would, therefore, be surprising, if the reactions of overseas students to their experiences in a university were not beset with at least some problems, simply because, in the process of being accepted, they will have been subjected to various stages of determination of their status. Consequently, whatever the complications which surround the ordinary indigenous student, the position of the overseas student will be worse.

Although the enquiry on which this chapter is based took place in advance of the major changes in treatment already outlined, it became apparent very quickly that there were some problems of identifcation. Contacts with the Overseas Students Society at York provided a basis for initial discussions about the kinds of areas of concern which might be significant. These early informal contacts also indicated that an interpretive enquiry would be warranted. Arrangements were, therefore, made to identify overseas students in order to organise a series of interviews. This was done from the official University register. The first letters of approach brought a number of replies to the effect that the respondents were not overseas students even though they held a foreign passport.

Most of these said that they had lived in Britain for over five years prior to entering the University. Other students with foreign passports had been borne and effectively brought up in this country. There were, in addition, students holding

British passports who had spent most of their lives abroad because of their parents' work and who, in the context of adapting to a strange environment, could conceivably be held to justify being treated as overseas students. It is not that these distinctions are confused in what were the various official guidelines. The existence of these different groups did, however, serve to emphasise that too many assumptions should not be made about the perceptions of such students, nor about the kinds of experiences they might have. This was also taken as further evidence to support the intention of carrying out informal interviews with students rather than adopting a more pre-determined research strategy.

Other sources of caution came from initial contacts and covered such things as - ensuring that any potential interviewees understood the purpose of the enquiry: exploring reasons for choosing both the country and university of study; attitudes to other students, both overseas and indigenous; future intentions. Any and all of these were, it was suggested, likely to be very different, in many cases, as compared with equivalent reactions from indigenous students. The first of the above points was repeatedly stressed, usually on the grounds of ensuring anonymity to respondents, and mention was sometimes made of the possibility that some overseas students had had experience of their own countries monitoring their activities.

Two further points need to be mentioned before presenting the findings. This was an exploratory study in two ways: it was the first major independent research conducted by the author; it was also an approach to students which, at the time, had few published examples to provide much in the way of helpful guidelines. The predominant tradition of work in the area of motivation and expectation was essentially quantitative, via questionnaire methods of data collection. This was not only generally true in respect of research into students, but particularly true also in relation to the few studies of overseas students.

Of these, the major NFER study by Sen (1970) was not only typical, but also produced additional evidence which further influenced decisions about this enquiry. Sen conducted a sample survey, based initially on questionnaires coupled with a formal standardised test of proficiency in English. This stage was followed by personal interviews with a sub-sample, and the enquiry was completed with later information on eventual student performance. Contrasting the findings of the questionnaire and interview phases, Sen found that many students tended to minimise, or even omit, reference to any difficulties encountered in answering written questions. It was only during the interviews that such evidence emerged.

As with other studies, though - for example, those reported by Morris (1967) and Currie and Leggett (1965) - Sen was also concerned with successful completion of courses, as measured by formal results. Each of these enquiries seemed to focus attention on factors which appeared to correlate with non-completion or lower results than anticipated. There was much concern, therefore, with the views of those in official positions responsible for the courses the students were taking, and also with the ways in which the British Council made attempts to help students from overseas. Questionnaire approaches were ruled out as a result of examining the above reports.

Participant observation, though having many attractions, was also seen to be inappropriate to the situation of an indigenous student enquiring into the experiences of those from overseas. Criticism of interviews by some adherents to the observational paradigm - notably Cicourel (1964) - was taken to be less significant in the context of an exploratory enquiry than would have been the case for a more widespread investigation.

One interesting point which emerged from practice interviews, and which took on great significance in the actual enquiry, involved the problem of language. It appeared to be the case that even two students from the same country, separated only by a couple of hundred miles, can have difficulties in understanding and interpreting their own language. Understanding was added to the list of factors which should not be taken for granted, and also provoked the decision to use a tape-recorder - with each interviewee's permission and a pledge of anonymity and erasure after transcription. The extent of each eventual interview - most ran well over the anticipated half an hour towards an hour's duration - and the interest in the issues shown by the interviewees are taken as evidence that the presence of the tape-recorder did not unduly influence their reactions. All students seen were very forthcoming - not only in areas anticipated as a result of initial soundings - and initiated discussions in many other areas of concern.

The overall feeling is that the information

which emerged is reasonably representative of the experiences of overseas students at York. However, this is not therefore to say that such information can necessarily be generalised to cover all overseas students at all universities. York, for example, has relatively few overseas students. The adjacent city is also relatively small and has only a limited population of immigrant origins. However, where connections can be made with other studies, and similar findings emerge, there does exist a degree of justification for generalising beyond the specific context of the University of York.

Mention has already been made of the initial problem of identifying overseas students from the official university lists in order to arrange interviews. It was eventually decided to interview only those students who held foreign passports and who had, until entry to York - whether as undergraduate or postgraduate students - spent their life abroad. A sample of one-third of those so identified was chosen and stratified in such a way as to represent the main countries of origin of York overseas students, the areas of study and gender balance of the total group. In this latter respect it is clear that men dominate the scene for overseas students to a very significant extent - a feature generally reported in all such enquiries. For York the respective proportions were 69% men and 31% women for the whole group, and 74% men and 26& women at postgraduate level. All five main continents were represented but agreement to be interviewed was less forthcoming from students of African origin as compared with the remainder. To this extent, therefore, the replies are marginally unrepresentative of the total group of overseas students at York.

One major issue dominated the interviews - as it had done in the larger national enquiries of Morris (1967) and Sen (1970). This was the problem of acclimatisation to the new institution, and within this main area of concern language became the main focal point of discussion. Before going on to examine the completely unanticipated results which emerged in this context, we shall examine the other outcomes in order to provide a background to the issues of greatest importance.

A distinction which needs to be made immediately is that between undergraduates and postgraduates. The former tended, like studies of their indigenous counterparts have suggested, to see entry to university as part of a natural progression of education. The latter tended to be more functionally concerned with future job implications of their studies, and many of them were, in fact, sponsored by their home governments in some way or another.

There were also distinctions between the same two groups in terms of their choice of Britain in which to study. The undergraduates were more varied, with responses ranging between a fanatical following of British pop music and a desire to be part of this scene, through those for whom there were no university outlets at home - because of the absence of a university sector of education, or of a colour barrier to easy university access - to those for whom the relatively short length of British undergraduate courses was a significant attraction when set against the longer courses available in other countries. There was also the occasional student - each of whom, incidentally, admitted to substantial disillusionment with these ideas at the time of interview - who had obviously grown up indoctrinated into some kind of Commonwealth view of Britain as a kind of Utopia. "I thought it was going to be Canaan, the Promised Land", was how one of these put it. At the time of the interviews - in advance of the decision to charge full-cost fees - about half of the undergraduates interviewed said that they had explored a choice between Britain and the United States and had been swayed towards Britain on cost grounds. The implications of the change in government policy are obvious.

For the postgraduate group, there was again evidence of a lack of equivalent opportunity at home for many students, but this was usually coupled with some knowledge of the specialist tuition or expertise available at York, which had been a positive attraction. Most also indicated that, on their return home, they would acquire prestige with a British postgraduate qualification and probable enhancement of job prospects.

The sources of both the general information about study in Britain, and the more detailed information which influenced decisions to study at York, came, predominantly, by word of mouth - sometimes, but only rarely enhanced by formal published information. Hardly anyone indicated the reverse process. It was apparent that while the majority of the students had made attempts - sometimes, but not always, successful - to acquire formal information, they generally felt that such information as they could obtain was not really adequate. In one case it was six years old. Official sources included the British Council, British Embassies,

Being an Overseas Student

Libraries and British education publications.
It seems clear, on this evidence, that the most effective recruitment agent for overseas students is the person who has already broken the ground, taken courses and gone back to say that the university or the course is good. This can be taken as an indication of the kind of immeasurable good-will which teaching overseas students can generate, and which reductions in the numbers of overseas students coming to Britain will eventually curtail. Of course, such sources are double-edged, since it is unlikely that information about unsatisfactory courses or institutions would work towards maintaining a constant stream of successor students. However, if word of mouth plays as significant a part in recruitment as this information would indicate, it clearly places a premium on the host institutions/departments to do everything possible to make the student's stay a satisfying one. It would also appear that, given the wide spread of countries of origin of the relatively small number of overseas students which York gets each year, it would be difficult - and very questionable in cost-effectiveness terms - to contemplate providing sufficient and detailed documentary information to satisfy the needs of all potential applicants from around the world.
Other factors, like the smallness of the University, the convenience and accessibility of the parent city, the historic nature of York itself, the relatively rural situation of the campus, and the availability of residential accommodation were all mentioned within the interviews as providing reasons for the particular choice of York once the decision to study in Britain had been made. In each case, however, the existence of these factors served not only to indicate the variety of dimensions involved in individual decisions, but also provided further evidence that the main source of information on these points was the informal grapevine. It is of interest to note that the reasons alluded to above would seem to be broadly identical with the cluster of factors which any indigenous student might offer in the same context. The University itself ensures that information on most of these factors is given prominence in the annual prospectuses it produces.
Expectations of their university experience tended to focus on courses and academic staff, with very little apparent concern for social life. Expectations of courses had two dimensions. On the

one hand was an assumption of high quality on the
part of most of the students - which matched well
their expressed reasons for wanting to study in
Britain. On the other hand - and this was much more
in evidence amongst the postgraduate students -
there was also a tendency to make comparisons with
experience in their own countries. In this latter
respect there was some evidence that British courses,
with their premium on reflection, argument and independent study - where the seminar rather than the
lecture forms the major learning context - are seen
as less well organised than overseas experience.
An odd example of a reversal of assumptions!
Organisation and specified curricula become major
criteria for course evaluation rather than the personal benefits which might accrue. However, the
above views must be set against the general appreciation of these students of the approachability of
academic staff. These were seen to be less god-
like and appearing to be more concerned with the
individual student than had been expected. Here
again, though, there were indications of variation
in student reactions to the same situations and
dictated by prior experience. For example, a
Greek and an American student, at the same stage of
reading for the same degree in the same department
commented, respectively: "I found the staff very
helpful and not like the 'baronial' professors at
home who are very high and don't talk to students",
(G); and "I was most disappointed with the lack of
concern for students shown by the faculty. I was
almost being begged to learn when I was in the
States", (A).

    The evidence of the effects of previous exper-
ience in determining expectations, and colouring
perceptions, of the University may be little more
than what common-sense would dictate. Perhaps the
only significant and unexpected outcome of this
initial stage of the analysis was the evidence of
the use of informal personal contacts and a kind of
grapevine as the key source of information which
influenced the decisions to come to Britain and to
a particular university.

    Lewis and Vulliamy (1978) have shown very
clearly that undergraduate students make use of their
own extensive grapevine to pass on informal information about courses, and that such information is
more likely to be used by students in making course
choices than any formal and official departmental
arrangements. The existence, in this different
context of overseas students, of a similar and influ-

ential informal ad hoc network must be taken as further evidence of the need to ensure a wider concern for understanding - which can only be based on direct contacts - of the nature of the student experience and the factors which affect student perceptions. Without such understanding, two things are likely to continue: official information will continue to be misleading, presenting, as it does, only the academic perspective on a given situation; and official information will become increasingly irrelevant to most aspects of student decision-making. Either or both of these outcomes cannot but work to the disadvantage of the institution.

At the same time, and returning to the specific context of the overseas students, the evidence presented of the varied perceptions to the same course experiences and relationships, suggests that if departments/universities wish to maintain or strengthen links with students from abroad, they need to ensure that those completing their courses return home in a position to retail glowing recommendations. To this end it is even more imperative that academics become aware of the major dimensions of the experiences of overseas students. We shall go on to show that these lie in the social domain rather than within the narrow confines of academic contexts.

As was indicated earlier, language was the main problem on which students focused in the interviews. While, at a superficial level, this might be expected, the content and nature of their comments was entirely unexpected. Equally unexpected were the implications of the comments these students made and which bear significantly on the need to ensure that students return home able to transmit positive reactions to later enquirers. The main point is best illustrated with quotations.

> Our language is quite a bit different -
> it doesn't matter what we do, you have
> phrases and words which are completely
> foreign to us. People don't realise how
> great the problem is. (Canadian postgraduate)

> The range of accents mades me feel very
> much in a foreign country. (American
> undergraduate)

> Because I thought to know more English than
> I could, I was so quite disappointed because
> I couldn't talk. (Greek postgraduate)

> We used language as an alibi. There were other difficulties of communication, but we blamed language. (Italian postgraduate)
>
> I am thinking that I am a bit lost in the campus. The people I thought were strange - I couldn't cope with them. (Greek undergraduate)
>
> You are not interested in the same things. it is easy for you, you are only concerned about what to eat or what to do in the evenings. You do not have any interest in the state of the world. (South American undergraduate)
>
> Being a foreigner, I expected people to come to me - but no-one did, so I decided I had to make the first move. (Dutch undergraduate)
>
> In common ordinary people there is no racial superiority, but I have found it here among intellectual snobs. (Indian postgraduate)
>
> People seem to suspect you, or ignore you, or view you as some sort of strange creature. You feel uncertain what is going to happen. (African postgraduate)
>
> I could hardly buy the tickets to York when I arrived because of the language. (Asian postgraduate)

The only group of students for whom there was no admission of any language problems contained those from Australia and New Zealand. Their main concern was adapting to the British climate - buying a pullover for the first time in his life (an Australian student), or having 'flu. five times in his first term at York - which was the unhappy experience of a New Zealand student. This last point, though, was not peculiar to the antipodean group, and affected a substantial majority of students from countries with climates significantly different from ours.

The interviews indicated that language was perceived to be a major barrier to effective socialisation into the main student body. However, even from the above quotations, it can be seen that the problem is not simply one of language, but more of a general cultural phenomenon for which language becomes the main indicator. Language is, after all, a cultural device, and shades of added meanings and subtle shifts of interpretation are associated both with the words themselves, and also with their associated contexts and other elements of non-verbal communication.

Whilst extreme examples were not common to all students, the majority of them - and even including those (like North Americans) for whom a variant of English is the first language - had experienced a total situation which gradually imposed a degree of social apartheid upon them. Following some form of culture shock on arrival, perhaps exaggerated by some form of language difficulties, they arrive at a new campus to find that the majority of students - the indigenous ones - not only appear (falsely perhaps) at home and at ease, but also present an appearance of indifference to these newcomers. The only friendly faces appear to be those similarly placed in a foreign environment, with whom experiences and common concerns can be shared.

The lack of integration, coupled with the necessity to find human contacts with other overseas students, promotes an inward-looking attitude and a significant lack of opportunity to enlarge on a facility to use English in communication. The similar situation through which the indigenous newcomers have also passed (see Chapter 2) has also provided them with their own established groups of friends and contacts which tend not to incorporate any overseas members. The two isolated groups are thus locked into their own separate networks, and the gulf between them presents an increasingly impenetrable barrier. The overseas students' perceived diminished competence in English, coupled with their perceptions of the indigenous students reinforcing the stereotype of the reserved Britisher, reduces confidence in being able to cope with the normal demands of social interaction. A vicious circle is established and becomes self-sustaining. Patterns like this seem to become established quite quickly. Most of the students interviewed reckoned that it had all happened rapidly, and that the circle of impenetrability was complete well before the ending of their first term at York. If changes are to be made they must, in consequence, be made early and quickly.

It is worth adding here that the author has an impression - which it has to be admitted would be difficult to support in any kind of quantitative way, but which resulted from the experience of the interviews reinforced by the transcription of the tapes - that there was some difference on this issue for undergraduates and postgraduates. The problem seemed most acute for the postgraduates. Though whether this results from the much smaller group of undergraduates, who therefore had less of a basis for sticking together, is open to question. It is also conceivable that undergraduates had heavier timetables, and were forced into functional contacts with indigenous students to a greater extent than might have been the case for postgraduates. Most postgraduates might have been expected to be engaged in individual research work, which could also have served to increase their isolation. Postgraduates, too, were older, in general, than the undergraduates, and many had left families behind and anticipated lengthy absences from them; another example, perhaps, of the distinction between the 'really mature' and the younger students, which Rothschild discusses in Chapter 4.

Whatever the reasons for the need for social contact, the desire for it might be more pressing, and its absence could have been more noticeable. Previous university experience in the home country - already identified as a source of difference - is a major influence on the perceptions of their British experience, and would be likely to play a greater part for postgraduates.

In addition to the enforced isolation of these overseas students, and the role of language as a major source and indicator of the problem, one further aspect also emerged from these interviews. This concerned the substantial difference between the problems of social integration created and enhanced by language difficulties, and the apparent lack of similar problems in the formal context of learning. Had this issue not emerged in many of the interviews, the implications of the material already presented could give rise to the conclusion that these overseas students must have found great difficulty in coping with the language demands of the courses they were following. It might, for example, be argued, with reasonable justification, that the nature of language used in high levels of education is conceivably more complex and demanding than that used in ordinary discourse. Presumably - and without going into detail in terms of linguistic analysis - there is at least a common-sense view that one hall-mark of higher education is a tendency towards abstract thinking and complex conceptual analysis.

Being an Overseas Student

Even if such a common-sense view has any substance, the evidence from these students showed that, from their point of view, there was far less of a concern with coping with the demands of their academic courses. There were one or two exceptions to this, but the vast majority of the students said that they experienced few difficulties in processing material presented in lectures, accommodating to the heavy demands of lengthy reading lists, participating in seminars, or writing essays which appeared to reach satisfactory levels in terms of supervisory reactions.

Even in the case of the few exceptions to this general picture, the bulk of any disconcerting experiences which presented language problems emerged in the first few weeks and seemed to be closely associated with other factors. These contextual factors included problems in coming to terms with a different pattern of student/lecturer relationship than was expected or had previously been experienced. Such evidence reinforces the earlier conclusion about the impact on perceptions of previous educational experience. Where students had experienced learning in contexts which were very one-sided, and where they were not accustomed to being treated in sociable terms by faculty staff, it is not surprising that their settling in periods were rather difficult. It is also possible that the language barrier could be perceived as creating the problem which, in fact, lay elsewhere.

Such difficulties as were mentioned, and which were seen to be related to the academic context of learning, again reflected cultural assumptions embedded in discourse and ideas. For example, overseas students of Education referred to the unexamined differences between the systems they had experienced and the systems they were expected to analyse. Issues concerning the mechanism through which social class appears to be closely related to educational opportunity do not translate easily to a country in which universal education does not exist. Similarly, the study of the economics of developed, industrialised countries with a substantial and strong monetary system carries with it, in such countries, many assumptions with which it is taken for granted that many readers of the relevant texts will be familiar. Such assumptions will cover vocabulary, as well as the parameters and concepts through which the analysis is developed. These may not have much concrete meaning to a student from a third world country where different assumptions operate.

The situation for science students and for postgraduate research students was less extreme than the above picture suggests. There is a universality to the content and concepts of science. Research students have already, and almost by definition of their position, mastered more than satisfactorily the rudiments of their chosen disciplines, and are beginning to focus on specialised issues. Again we can see the pervasiveness of background experience and its influence on attitudes and expectations. Technical problems of reading text-books, writing an essay in language not one's own, following and engaging in arguments, presented few problems for most students interviewed. Where, however, the subject matter of a course was rooted in evidence from countries with significant differences from a student's country of origin, the 'hidden curriculum' of the language of discourse did present major problems of accommodating to and meeting course demands.

Whilst this was sometimes perceived by students as just another part of the general language problem they faced, the evidence they presented indicated that mastery of language at the surface level was not the real problem. It is the shades of meaning which are taken for granted by native speakers, and which are part of the social experience of growing up and learning the language and the embedded concepts it represents, which are lacking for many students from overseas. Only practice, through extensive contact with indigenous speakers can ameliorate this problem.

These academic experiences, where they occur, serve to reinforce the isolation already felt in more informal and social aspects of the University. They add, therefore, to the difficulties encountered in becoming a full and equal member of the University community. Although they were not experienced by the majority of overseas students, it was felt to be of sufficient importance to warrant examining the faculty view. To this end, some informal discussions were held with academic staff after the student interviews. While these interviews were in no sense representative, they do indicate a situation which suggests a lack of a complete appreciation of the problems of overseas students.

The academic staff chosen had all been involved in teaching overseas students in a number of contexts at undergraduate and/or postgraduate levels - some were involved with the students already iinterviewed. Generally they valued the presence of overseas students and felt that they coped more than adequately with what was perceived of as a more difficult situation than that faced by their indigenous peers. In addition, though, there was an equally general view that overseas students had significant language problems to face in coping with their courses, and these added to their other difficulties in accommodating to strange circumstances, situations and experiences.

What is of interest here is that the staff perception of the language problems of overseas students was rather different from those represented by the students and described above. From the faculty point of view, the problems were at the surface level - concerned with vocabulary, spelling, grammar, and syntax. There was no mention of the cultural assumptions built into the structure of knowledge put over in their courses. The only factor to emerge from these limited staff discussions, and which seems to have any bearing on the students' own perceptions, was a concern that overseas students seemed rather withdrawn in the relatively informal settings of seminars and tutorials. They were seen to have problems in participating as freely and readily as the majority of indigenous students. Again, the evidence was interpreted as resulting from lack of adequate mastery of the language.

While the nature of the two sources of evidence are not at all directly comparable - the staff discussions were fairly short, much more directed to issues emerging from the student interviews, and scarcely representative of the totality of staff experience - nonetheless, unless they were completely untypical, their responses do provide some basis for raising the issue of the major difference of interpretation of common experience.

From the students' point of view, there were few qualms about their competence to handle the basic language of learning in their particular discipline. What they felt to be a problem lay in the area of contextual matters underlying the surface language, or assumed in the nature of the analyses presented. Such a situation was more extreme for contextually varied subjects in the arts and social sciences, and far less noticeable in the sciences. It can also be added that if these students are anything like their predecessors from overseas, they will demonstrate their mastery of the essential language of discourse in the successful completion of their course requirements. It is, effectively, the social dimension of language which creates barriers to integration, especially at the informal level of contacts with the majority indigenous student population. The lack of opportunities for practice in colloquial English, which this absence of contact creates, serves to exaggerate further the sense of isolation and, as time moves on, makes it more difficult to break the barriers down.

From the staff perspective, these students appear to have language problems within the area of work, and any sign of withdrawal, or non-participation in group learning situations, is taken as an indicator of linguistic difficulty. The worst possible interpretation which can be offered here is that of staff insensitivity, which entails both the missing of evidence of capacity to cope with the linguistic demands of the discipline, as well as the misinterpretation of withdrawal as indicating linguistic incompetence rather than social insecurity. At best, the evidence can only be taken to indicate some lack of concern with the social dimensions of the student experience, and any implications this might have for effective involvement in the narrow academic sphere. From this point of view we assume that the total world of the student involves inter-relationship between all the contributory and apparently separate parts. Personality, intellect, aspirations, expectations, past experience, social relationships and the learning milieu interact in a variety of ways to affect each other and, in combination. to constrain and define the overall experience of being a student.

In this respect, therefore, students from overseas show similarities with the experiences of indigenous students, even though their circumstances are clearly very different, and the consequences show signs of major variations in what is eventually experienced. The major implication is that we cannot treat as independent the student experience in the formal academic context. Evidence of performance, and capacity to deal with the many differing requirements which courses demand, are affected in very significant ways by factors external to the context of learning. The problems experienced in the social dimensions of student life, for overseas students, clearly has a major impact on their capacity to identify with other students and make relationships with them as part of the University community. The absence of significant social contacts forces overseas students back on themselves, and

Being an Overseas Student

creates the appearance, eventually, of lack of involvement within learning. Although the consequences are different, and the situations they experience are not at all the same, there can be no grounds for presuming that the same general principles do not apply to all students.

If this is the case, it makes a strong argument for ensuring that faculty make themselves aware of factors within the totality of student experience, and how these can manifest themselves in the ways in which students face problems in accommodating to the demands of their courses.

Overseas students survive their foreign university experience. It is also evident that enough of them return home with glowing reports of their experiences to ensure that, other circumstances permitting, a continual stream of future students will follow them. What is of concern, and has been highlighted by this small enquiry, is the possibility of increasing the benefits of their experiences. Such increases will operate in two directions. Overseas students could be encouraged towards a greater integration and involvement with their indigenous peers - with benefits of increased linguistic competence, a greater feeling of belonging to the University community, a consequent capacity to make more of the opportunities for engaging in discussion within their courses, and a better understanding of the nuances of British culture through greater involvement and wider language appreciation. In addition, indigenous students would also benefit from having new groups of students with whom to widen their own experience of the world, and through becoming aware of alternative perspectives, experiences and cultures from other parts of the world.

It is possible to speculate that the situation of the University of York - being relatively small, with a close campus community situated near a small and pleasant city with few significant social problems - ensures that the kind of isolation experienced by these students is far less than that which might occur in much larger universities associated with the major conurbation. If this is the case, the experiences of the vast majority of overseas students who come to Britain must be much worse than those described in this chapter. The improvements which could be brought about through greater understanding in such cases must, therefore, also be greater. When the future of overseas students as a major feature of our higher education system is increasingly at risk because of political decisions concerning finance and identity, it becomes of greatest importance to ensure that those who do arrive are encouraged to gain the maximum benefit from their hard-won opportunity. Both faculty and indigenous students have a major responsibility for ensuring that this is done. It will, however, only happen if their hosts recognise the nature of the problems which these visitors face. Critical to an understanding of this nature is its social and personal dimension.

Our findings provide no basis for large-scale institutional responses, or more administrative induction arrangements. These are only likely to exacerbate the difficulties by singling out the overseas students, and making them the centre of attention, when what they really seem to want is to blend into the University community and become indistinguishable from the majority of home-based students. Solutions, therefore, are best seen as the individual and personal responsibility of faculty staff - who attract and select the overseas students and eventually teach them - and their fellow students - who need to recognise that, like themselves, these students, too, need friendship and human contact in order to make the social dimension of their university experience as satisfying as the academic side will ultimately become functionally valued.

A last point needs to be made to close this chapter. This reflects the style of enquiry from which these findings have emerged. Mention was made, at the beginning, of the large-scale, predominantly questionnaire-based approaches of others to the problems of overseas students. Nothing reported in this chapter contradicts any of the conclusions reported elsewhere. In fact, most of the major findings are demonstrably consistent with other large-scale studies, and this has allowed a greater degree of generalisation than might normally have been the case. However, it is argued that the central findings which we have introduced - on the social and cultural dimensions of the language problem of overseas students - could only have emerged from personal discussions of a free-ranging kind. To this extent, therefore, this enquiry has two implications. One at the substantive level of providing insights into the world of the overseas students in Britain; the other at the procedural level of demonstrating the benefits of an open-ended, interpretive approach.

Chapter 6

BEING A WOMAN PHYSICS STUDENT

A full account of this study is available elsewhere (Lewis, 1983), and a number of the findings will not be examined here. It is important, though, to provide a general account of the origins and intentions behind the study so that the comments and interpretations which are made in this chapter can be set in their proper context.

Three things conspired to produce a focus of attention on the educastional experiences at university of women physics students. One was the general concern of the author with student experiences in higher education - which this book reflects. Another was a series of fortuitous circumstances within the Education Department at York which resulted in the author having close working relationships with colleagues and students in the Physics Department. Some of these contacts involved spending time in the teaching laboratories in which it became rapidly noticeable that there were very few women students, and that they did not appear to mix freely with the men students in the social interchange surrounding the experimental work. Consideration of these factors led to a growing interest in the increasing numbers of publications bearing on the clearly differentiated experience of women in education generally.

Putting the three things together produced the idea that it would be worthwhile to try to interview, informally, all the women undergraduates taking physics in one academic year. The numbers involved - see below - made this a realistic possibility and, with the permission of the Head of the Physics Department, arrangements were made for the interviews to take place at mutually convenient times throughout the year. For convenience, and also because it was felt that there might be definable differences as students enlarged their university experiences, students in each year group were interviewed separately.

As with the other examples of student experience reported in previous chapters, this enquiry also called into questioin a number of taken for granted assumptions. Some of these concerned the consequences to the students, as women, of operating in a predominantly masculine world of physics. Others, with which we shall predominantly be concerned here, add further detail to the general picture being established of the nature of the student experience and, significantly, raise serious questions about the image of university life which these women acquired. Because the original impetus for the enquiry reflected an interest in these students' experiences of physics, we shall offer some comment on this aspect before developing the main lines of argument.

The bulk of recent studies of women's experiences in education - ranging from the more general, e.g. Byrne (1978) and Deem (1978), to the highly specific, like Kelly (1981a) - seemed to indicate a number of key issues. One of these was that physics was perceived as a predominantly 'masculine' subject. This notion of masculinity appeared to be predicated on two grounds: that, as schooling progresses, fewer and fewer girls continue with the study of physics; further, that in doing so, girls are presented with a dilemma between maintaining their feminine identities or becoming closely identified with the study of physics.

Kelly (1981b) has illustrated the first of these points in the following way: the number of boys studying physics at various levels, for every girl at the same level, is

Attempting O level	3.8
Attempting A level	4.9
On Advanced F.E. Courses	13.1
Obtaining first degree	7.2
Doing graduate work	9.6
Getting Ph.D.	17.1

These figures, as Kelly shows, present a much more extreme picture than those for any other science or mathematics subject. One dimension of the masculinity of physics, then, is simply represented by the high proportion of boys and men studying the subject.

For the second aspect, a number of papers can

be cited. Smithers and Collings (1981), in a study of 1900 lower sixth-form students, found that girls studying the physical sciences expressed attitudes and possessed expectations which were similar to those of similar male students. Weinreich-Haste (1978a, b, and 1981) has also suggested that the perceived masculinity of physics creates problems for girls who have ability but who, in making decisions about continuing to study the subject, are faced with a conflict between "an overt curriculum of achievement and a hidden curriculum of ... 'appropriate' characteristics and qualities for womanhood."

At the same time, other writers, e.g. Head (1980), have demonstrated that neither cognitive differences between the genders, nor institutional factors to do with the organisation of schooling, are satisfactory explanations of this significant differentiation in the numbers of men and women studying the physical sciences. The same author (Head, 1981) has also argued that the traditional approach to many studies of women's education has been via quantitative and psychometric methods, and that these may not be the best tools for such enquiries. The argument indicates that, if we are to explore the actual and perceived experiences of students, it may be better to work from their views rather than to try to squeeze them into some predetermined mould through questionnaires and attitude inventories. Such approaches might allow for very adequate descriptions but, by their nature, could easily fail to provide any basis for an explanation of what is being described. It also follows that, if the wrong questions are asked, misleading descriptions could readily ensue.

Because of these arguments, it was felt that the approach to the women physics students at York should be through unstructured interviews. Four explicit questions were used in each interview - concerned with the type of school attended, choices of subjects at O and A level, choice of university courses and future career expectations. These were intended to provide a basis of factual information, but also to allow for more extensive discussion of views which the students held about influences on their decisions, or comments on their experiences. Each interview was prefaced by an invitation to agree to the interview being unobtrusively tape-recorded, in order to allow the discussion to develop as an informal conversation without interruption for note-taking.

Being a Woman Physics Student

Individual interviews were arranged with all 33 of the women students reading physics on various kinds of undergraduate course, over the whole three-year period. There were 9 students in the first year, 16 in the second year and 8 in their final year. Only one interview failed to materialise - one second-year student did not respond. The 32 completed interviews can, therefore, be taken as reasonably representative of the total group even though there could be some grounds for arguing that the student may not be typical of women physics undergraduates nationally. For example, the Physics Department has consistently operated a very stringent policy of initial selection, with an average A level performance of 3 B grades being the normal requirement. No official policy exists to suggest any discrimination, either of a positive or a negative kind, in respect of the gender of applicants. It is of some interest, therefore, that the proportions of women students entering the Physics Department in each of the three years in question are marginally higher than the proportions of women applying for other courses.

In each of the three years under review, the respective proportions of male:female applicants was 86:14, 84:15, and 84:16. These figures compare very well with the national figures given in the annual UCCA reports, which give an average of 86:14 for each of these years. With total undergraduate entry being 41, 60 and 56 in each of the three years for all the possible physics courses, the male:female ratios were, respectively, 78:22, 72:28 and 84:16. There is, therefore, some suggestion that the quality of the women students was above average, within a department which operates on a principle of requiring a high level of ability for all its annual intake of undergraduates.

On the question of the particularity of these York students, a larger study by Walton (1982) in London has produced evidence of very similar findings. This can be taken as some indication that the situations and experiences described owe more to general factors than they do to any special features either of the Physics Department or of the University of York.

Rothschild (in Chapter 4) has already drawn attention to a potential source of difference between science and arts students in terms of the variation in personal freedom allowed by time-tabling constraints. We can add another source of variation here. For York in general, the male:

Being a Woman Physics Student

female ratio has been fairly static at around 55:44 in recent years. The Physics Department, therefore, can be seen as one of the contributors to the male preponderance within a university in which the numbers of women undergraduates (see Chapter 1) is somewhat higher than the national average. This chapter, therefore, deals with aspects of the experiences of a particular sub-group of students, and some of the information will indicate differences between these and other students. More important, though, will be any signs which make links with the material presented in previous chapters and which would indicate something about the nature of these women's experiences qua student. We start, though, with an issue which has strong gender connections.

The issue arose spontaneously in the first few interviews completed and, as a result, a deliberate attempt was made in the subsequent interviews to make sure the point was covered. In most of these later cases it was not necessary, as it also emerged spontaneously and can, therefore, be taken as something which is at the forefront of these women's reflections on their education.

Only 2 of the 32 students expressed any surprise at the relative smallness of the numbers of women students in their University classes. All the others expected such a situation and, if they made any comment about it, this was usually to the effect that an even smaller proportion of women had been anticipated. The two atypical comments were based, in one case on a general expectation, coloured by a correct view of the University - that it has a reputation for a more equal balance of the genders than many - that there would be more physics students who were women. In the other case, the student drew on her own experience in a Sixth Form College, where a small majority of the A level physics group had been girls.

What seems to emerge from this one point is evidence that these women students had some attitudes and expectations already affected by the previous school experience. Specifically, their experience had, for most of them, indicated that, by choosing to study physics at university, they were, with foreknowledge, entering an institutional framework in which they would form a tiny minority. At this stage, though, it would still be possible to see this as providing a basis for expecting that their attitudes and expectations in general might be identifiable with the majority of their male peers. It was on this last point that it was hoped that the series of interviews would shed some light. By focusing attention on that tiny minority of women students who had eventually made their way up the educational pyramid, their elaboration on their own experiences and perceptions could provide a basis for examining the implications of women continuing to demonstrate a high level of ability in physics.

To illustrate the further dimension of their school experience, 21 of the 32 students interviewed had attended a single sex school up to age 16, but for their sixth form education - which, in some cases, necessitated changing school - the balance changed markedly. 17 of the 32 completed their 16+ education in a single sex institution. Writers like Byrne (1978), Blackstone (1976) and Deem (1978) have already argued that, where girls are engaged in subject choice which has implications for gender identity, such decisions are much more likely to be fostered in single sex than in mixed schools. The argument, briefly, suggests that the equivalence between school and society in mixed schools allows prevailing social stereotypes to play a more significant part in determining boy and girl subject choices. Thus, boys would be less likely to choose 'feminine' subjects like home economics in mixed schools, and girls would be less likely, in similar circumstances, to choose technical drawing.

Similarly, because of the preponderance of the other gender in courses like languages, boys are less frequently to be found in these courses at more advanced levels. We have already seen that girls form decreasing minorities at the more advanced levels of science and mathematics courses.

We should note, too, that the number of single sex schools has significantly reduced in recent years, as the comprehensivisation of secondary education has gained ground. Not only were these new schools to break new ground in catering for the total ability range, they were also used, in many cases, as a vehicle for further social engineering, by reducing the segregation of the sexes, which was so common in the selective system. Given that the preponderance of single sex schools remains within the grammar and independent sectors of secondary education, and that these will continue to send a disproportionate number of students to universities, the surprise in the above figures must be at the relatively high proportion of women physics students which they reflect. There is, therefore, some support for the earlier comment, reported from Head

Being a Woman Physics Student

(1980), of the lack of significance to be attached to institutional influence in gender differentiation.

What remains, then, in terms of searches for potential explanations of the serious decline in numbers of women going on to more advanced levels of physics, are the factors associated with external social pressures - both within families, and in terms of peer relationships - and factors associated with the actual experiences of education.

In terms of the school experiences of these students, a number of factors stood out in their recollections. There was a view of physics as representing "orderliness", with "laws that you apply instead of fact that you have to learn", and that it has the reputation of being "seen as the hardest subject at school, and that you were thought to be very bright if you chose to do it." Comments like these, which were typical of the set of responses made by the group, were also coupled with more disturbing comments that "girls with ability still seem to opt for what they think are the easy subjects"; and "Where girls have a wide range of potential ability, they tend not to choose physics, because it is seen as a 'hard' subject and as a male preserve."

Such views were further elaborated in relation to the students' perspectives on their own situation, having chosen to take this 'hard' subject. Thus, "If a girl came out with an intelligent comment in class I'd think 'that's one up for our side', because we're conditioned from the start not to expect this." Or, "Men teachers at my school seemed to put people off. They used to say to girls, "don't worry if you find physics difficult, there are more important things in life than physics." And a comment made by one student, but echoed in similar vein by most of them when talking about their initial experiences at university. Talking about the normal exchange of information about one's subjects of study, she said that she was frequently met with the reaction that "You don't look like I'd expect a woman physicist to look like."

That the educational experience of women physics students is perceived as a battleground, is identified even more by comments reporting on their experiences once at York. "Sometimes I feel I don't want to let the side down, so I work hard to show I'm as good as them." "It wasn't until the Part I exam results came out and they could see that quite a few of us had done better than a lot of them, that the lads began to look at us as if we had something

115

after all."

Remarks like these, again typical of the range of responses from the total group, go some way towards giving an outline picture of what it is like to be a woman studying physics. It is done in the awakening knowledge that it is one of the hardest subjects to study, and one in which you will find yourself in a rapidly diminishing minority. In addition, many teachers seem to operate with a view that it is a subject which is scarcely appropriate to girls at all. This last aspect was made worse in many of the schools attended by these students - and in the light of national figures we are tempted to see this limited sample as representative - by three main features surrounding the critical periods of subject choice, at O and at A level.

Firstly schools - or at least these schools - offered choices at around thirteen in which it was easily possible not to take physics, thus allowing external influences and peer group pressures a large opportunity to work strongly against girls with ability and interest choosing to take it on. To do physics against such a background already indicates some special qualities about this minority of pupils. Secondly, there appeared to be a significant lack of useful advice from teachers about the implications for careers of many of the choices made. Thus, a number of these students commented adversely on their schools, both in terms of not being made aware of what they had eventually found to be a very wide range of career opportunities opening to them as a result of taking physics, and also in terms of their peers being allowed to go on with arts and language courses. In these latter cases, commenting on talking with such students at York, they found their own very clear ideas of eventual lines of development contrasted starkly with the apparent lack of opportunities available to arts students - whether male or female. To this extent, therefore, there is evidence here which supports two issues to which Rothschild has already drawn attention. The lack of sound advice for many students contemplating entry to university directly after school, and the difference in attitude between arts and science students in relation to career orientation. The combination of these two factors, when added to the students' evidence that there are many girls with potential ability who fail to follow a science programme, suggests that there is much which could be done to encourage greater numbers of students into sciences in higher education - to their own, and eventually

Being a woman Physics Student

to the benefit of industrial and technological development.

Ebbutt (1981) is amongst those who have drawn attention to another masculine dimension of physics. Not only is there a preponderance of men taking the subject, but the whole thrust of the hidden message transmitted by most physics text books re-emphasises this masculine domination. Applied examples are almost always chosen from areas which also have strong masculine connections - like engineering. Certain areas of physics are also seen to have strong links with outside activities which are also male-connected - like electronics and messing about with bikes and cars. Harding (1983) explores these and other factors which also influence girls' attitudes and school experiences.

A clear majority of the women students interviewed reported similar experiences in terms of finding that in some areas of physics it "would have been nice to see a woman in the picture in the text books doing something", or that "when we did electricity, a lot of the boys in class already knew about resistances and things from their hobbies." Their comments also showed that this kind of differentiation did not stop on entry to university. "In electronics, boys think it's their subject and girls don't really know how to do it, and shouldn't be there. In a practical a boy will sit down and get on with it and leave you waiting. They presume you don't know how to do it." Or, perhaps more plaintively, "Boys seem to take up electronics as a hobby and girls don't. What we do always seems new to me, but boys always seem to know it already. Nothing I do outside physics is relevant to physics at all."

A number of activities were identified by these women as examples of hobbies which their male fellow-students engaged in, and which were felt to have significant benefits in reinforcing both knowledge of physics, as well as encouraging experimental attitudes and dexterity - radio making, electronic circuitry and repairing cars and motor bikes were frequently mentioned. The women's interests, outside physics, covered a wider range of activities than they suggested were evidenced amongst their male peers. They included such things as music, listening to records and playing instruments, reading, theatre, both acting and visiting, horse-riding, sport, travelling, sewing and dancing.

If we put these things together at this stage, we find that not only are these women competing in a relatively alien environment, they seem to feel themselves doubly disadvantaged by the further differences they notice between themselves and their male counterparts. Men can draw from their outside experience and add to their understanding of their subject; women have to make do and cope with what is presented within their courses. Nothing of their outside interests appears to have demonstrable relevance to their courses. Few of their activities provide a basis for developing skills which can be used within their courses. Much of their course content comes new and is therefore relatively more difficult to comprehend than it is for men students who might be able to make connections with other experience and knowledge. Such a combination of circumstances add further weight to the earlier contention that women students have to exhibit special qualities of resilience and determination, as well as continuing to manifest high levels of academic performance, if they are to continue with their studies of physics.

What became more interesting to the author, though, was the fact that the women students felt that the men they worked with were at a significant disadvantage because of this overlap between their personal interests and their courses, and in spite of any functional benefits which could accrue from enhanced experience. It is this point that the remainder of this chapter will concentrate upon, since it is seen as having greater significance in the context of the whole collection of studies.

The perceived male disadvantage emerges first in the narrowness of focus which the women thought the 'boys' exemplified. Interesting also was the almost universal use of the term 'boy(s)' as a description of their fellow-students - who were, of course, men. We shall return to the implication of this usage, with its assumptions about delayed maturation, as the argument develops. On the issue of male disadvantage, one comment stands out, although many other students made reference to the same point. One student said, "It's as if they see nothing in life other than physics and they choose their outside interests on the basis of their interests in physics." Such a comment has another side in remarks like: "Well, I think that a university education should be a general education. It's not just as if we're here only to do physics, there are so many other things to do. We would become very narrow-minded if all we were interested in was our subject."

Being a Woman Physics Student

This view of university education as general education was universally shared by this group of students - and has certainly been found by other researchers, including much of the material reported by the Nuffield Group for Research and Innovation in Higher Education, and also recorded in Lewis and Vulliamy (1978) in their enquiry into the views of students taking combined degrees. This view, though, is one which the women felt that their male colleagues did not share. Here, for the first time. it is clear that there is a divergence from the accepted picture of women students as presented in other studies. For example, if we examine the picture reflected in the substantial enquiry of Smithers and Collings (1981), we find that girls studying the physical sciences in sixth forms are said to be very similar to boys. The sixth formers were highly introverted, not very outgoing, experienced substantial social difficulty in making relationships, and did not emphasise their femininity. Except on this last point - where comparison is not appropriate - Smithers and Collings found that the picture of the girls was identical with that produced for boys studying the physical sciences. Both groups bore a remarkable resemblance to the image of the conservative scientist put forward many years ago by Hudson (1966).

The women students reported on here were very much the opposite. They seemed anything but introverted, and on their own very well substantiated evidence were very outgoing, with a wide range of interests and a very broad spectrum of friends. As we have already noted, they also felt very strongly that the 'boys' with whom they worked exhibited very different characteristics. We must point out, though, that comparisons between the two sets of results are fraught with problems; not least in terms of the different research approaches adopted, and the very different samples of students involved in each case.

Other than in terms of the ways in which they reported being treated and reacted to by these 'boys' - particularly in laboratory sessions, but also occasionally in tutorials when it was reported that comments were made about the surprise expressed by 'lads' when a woman came up with a good answer - the women felt that they had not been subject to any other kind of discriminatory pressure, and certainly none was reported from the all male staff of the Physics Department. Nonetheless, as already mentioned, their impressions were coloured by the feeling

ing that they were working in a battlefield, in which the genders were the contending forces. It was vitally important for them to be seen to do well, to justify, in ways which they felt were clearly not seen to be significant by the men students, their presence in classes and in the department. Their motivation was therefore very high, and generated by a recognition of their gender identities. It was not for its own sake, but to show what "we" could do.

As with the situation of the overseas students, described in the previous chapter, these perceptions were the result of reaction to experience, and created barriers which reinforced the nature of that experience. The author's earlier comment about noticing the lack of mixing in the teaching laboratories can be brought in here. Women find all aspects of physics new. Their outside interests do not provide a basis of confidence and expertise with which to embark on experimental situations. 'Boys' seem to feel that they should not be present and, in any case, enthusiastically begin their experiments immediately and, when in difficulty, would be unlikely to talk things over with a women student. Women physics students are therefore forced together, both for social contact, as well as for functional support. The academic context reinforces the attitudes which serve to create the initial separation. As in many other circumstances, once a system of apartheid is established, the experiences which it generates reinforce the assumptions which underpin the segregation. It becomes difficult to see how such a system of enforced segregation will break down naturally.

Given the high level of motivation which the situation generated in the women students, it did not come as a surprise to find that when the degree results came out - long after the third year interviews had been completed - the level of performance for the 8 final year women was marginally better than that of the parallel group of men. Four of the women got an Upper Second or above, compared with 13 of the men. The remaining four women students got Lower Second class degrees, whereas the remaining men got 8 Lower Seconds, 6 Thirds and 2 Ordinary degrees between them.

A study such as this cannot, by its nature, expect to provide an answer to the question of the extent to which different levels of motivation contribute to an explanation of this set of results. It is felt to be important, though, to note that these results emerge for a small group of women who, from the age of about eleven, have been constantly attempting to demonstrate their abilities in an area of study which they have come to realise is hedged about with attitudes and expectations which work to their disadvantage, and to the advantage of their male counterparts. In addition, the social circumstances in which they have grown up have made them aware of a general feeling that they are somehow odd to be doing what they are, and that there are very few ways in which they can harness their outside interests to reinforce their understanding of physics.

To come through such an extended educational experience so successfully is to demonstrate a commitment to personal fulfilment very much beyond the normal. The general run of evidence on university students indicates that most of them operate within areas which fit the normal set of gender stereotypical expectations. Because of this it is seen as surprising that other large-scale studies of women's experiences in the sciences do not appear to have been able to differentiate male and female students. Indeed, in some cases, the findings go further and suggest an identity of characteristics, with women generally adapting to men's attitudes and aspirations when they move into essentially masculine areas of study.

In spite of the smallness of the sample involved here - counterbalanced by its consideration of the <u>total</u> group of women physics students who have emerged from the decimation of schooling - there would appear to be some justification for suggesting that women of high ability in the physical sciences are very unlikely to be differentiable from their male peers. If this is so, then further weight can perhaps be given to Head (1981) in his argument that, for studies in this area of female experience, we need to concentrate upon approaches which will uncover the students' own views. The corrollory could be that the very nature of large-scale quantitative studies has a tendency to hide the variation of individual differences from what must be a very small sub-group within any general sample. In addition, by operating with pre-determined categories which, because of the nature of the prior research upon which they build, do not themselves reflect the experiences of students, they serve to foster potential misconceptions.

However, discussions of the merits of various styles of research is not the main point of this chapter. In terms of a general concern already outlined in Chapter 1, though, it can at least be suggested, from the evidence used here, that the intention to allow the students to express their own views in a relatively unconstrained fashion should guide future research into student expectations. In asserting this view, we echo the conclusion drawn by Entwistle and Wilson (1977), who commented upon "The difficulty we experienced in extrapolating our statistical results into the real world of lecturers and students." Their response to the problem "was to draw on the interview data and inject a dose of intuition" (p. 168). At least in our case, the attempt has been explicitly made to draw out the real world of these women students, and rely on interpretation of their own words rather than intuition.

To conclude this chapter, we now add one further dimension to our analysis: the students' views about their futures beyond their undergraduate period.

On this point it became apparent that the nearer the students were to finishing their courses, the more specific they were about their intentions and expectations. However, even the first year students were quite explicit about seeing their study of physics as leading to occupational opportunities which were directly linked to their scientific inclinations. There was no vagueness here at all, even if there was not any specific reference to a particular kind of job. What became of compelling interest emerged only after completion of the third year interviews, when specificity was the order of the day.

Before outlining these results, we can note that this clear occupational orientation is in line with the findings which Rothschild has already presented. Science students, she discovered, were very clear about commitments to jobs, whereas arts students had few views at all about what might follow their undergraduate careers. We cannot comment on the comparison with arts students here, but can confirm the picture of science students as having, from the beginning of their undergraduate lives, a clear sense that their university course had functional, as well as personal benefits to offer. While this may look as if we are beginning to modify the earlier suggestion that men and women students need to be differentiated, it became clear that, as far as the women were concerned, they saw their view of the future as being very different

Being a Woman Physics Student

from that of their male peers.

The third year students, at the time of the interviews, were already engaged in applications and interviews for quite specific jobs, and also seemed to have a clear picture of the level of degree result they were anticipating - borne out in each case, as a later examination of the degree lists showed. It became quite natural to ask those who were expecting a high level result whether they had thought about an academic career, based on moving into further study after graduation. In every case the student was adamant that an academic future was not at all attractive, and that none of them was interested in the possibility of entering graduate study in this, or in any other Physics Department.

When pressed for reasons for this reaction, the kinds of comments made fitted neatly with other remarks, noted earlier, concerning their views about the experiences of their male peers. The women were all concerned with seeing the opportunity of university education as general education in addition to the specific and functional expansion of knowledge and skills. The parallels with the findings of Lewis and Vulliamy (1978), and of Ward (1977) - not to mention the findings of the Nuffield Group - are very marked. There clearly does exist a substantial proportion of university students whose view of university experience puts a premium on the educational side of higher education. We shall return to this in the remaining chapters.

For the women physics students, this view of general education had elements of social maturation. "It has helped me to grow up a lot through being forced to be responsible for everything." There were also elements of career specification. "We are encouraged to get vac. jobs in industry, and my experience last Summer was all I needed to confirm my ideas about wanting to do that kind of work." There were also elements of personal intellectual satisfaction involved. "I had always liked the way physics consisted of laws which could be applied in a range of situations, and I wanted to carry it further. I've enjoyed the experience in spite of the hard work." There are elements of clarification of personal identity. "I thought I was good at (physics) at school and I wanted to see how far I could go." Each quotation has been taken from a different interview, but each interview carried expressions of similar sentiments. In addition, there was frequently mention of how the above dimensions combined to ensure that the undergraduate experience was prevented from remaining narrowly academic. "I've found the experience of being at university for three years a great opportunity to widen my horizons and meet new people and try new things. I think I'm a much more interesting person now."

Such remarks - which came through most forcibly from the third year students, and which were made rather more conditionally by the students of the other years - contrast markedly with the comments they made about their male contemporaries and the idea of staying on at university. "I couldn't possibly stay here any longer. It's been a good three years, but universities are so much out of contact with the real world that I couldn't possibly stay on." Another student said, "I wanted a job which would let me use my knowledge in dealing with real problems, and I don't think academic research would so this." Others added, "It's the boys who seem to want to stay on here and do research. I think they're afraid to get out into the real world", and "Research seems to be something that only the lads want to do. They don't seem to have any ideas outside that."

If we try to make sense of comments like these, it is difficult to detach them from the almost wholly male environment within which most of these women's advanced study of physics has taken place. In addition, we can incorporate the point of view expressed earlier about the wholly masculine perspective which the hidden curriculum of physics purveys. While these women have demonstrated their capacity not only to survive but also to prosper in such an environment, it is clear that they do not see the prospect of a life spent in such an environment at all attractive.

It is, however, possible to go a little further even than this, by incorporating the reactions to these women's experiences in trying to get jobs in equally male-dominated scientific industries. Detailed comments have been made about discrimination in Lewis (1983), so here we shall simply introduce the fact that it is more than the maleness of the institution which lies behind the disinclination of women to contemplate an academic career in physics. A number of them, after all, were going to work in research and development, so it cannot be advanced academic enquiry which is off-putting. Their job interview experience had reinforced for many of them, their general awareness that the kinds

Being a Woman Physics Student

of industries they might enter were as masculine - if not even more so - in terms of obvious and covert discriminatory attitudes as the University Physics Department. We have already seen that, in the department, it was fellow students rather than staff who offered any overt signs of discrimination.

For these kinds of reasons, therefore, it is felt that the prevalence of comments about the 'unreality' of the university experience, and the need to exchange it for contact with the 'real' world is the key to understanding the nature of these students' reactions. Their views indicate that they found substantial value in being detached for three years while they grew to full appreciation of themselves and their personal qualities. However, now that metamorphosis into a fully-fledged and qualified scientist is complete, the field of action has to move elsewhere. The University is, in this perspective, a place in which mature adults cannot be expected to live out fulfilled lives. Only the 'lads', who are generally perceived as immature - by implication, if not always explicitly - can satisfactorily contemplate remaining with the confines of a detached institution, thereby remaining out of touch with what women perceive to be real problems and real concerns. The constant use of the term 'boys' and 'lads' can, from this point of view, be seen to take on a further symbolic meaning, by drawing attention to the presumed immaturity of this majority group of adult students. 'Lads' hope to stay at university, and, by doing so, will remain as 'lads' for the foreseeable future. Postgraduate experience thus becomes the locus for even further deferred adolescence.

It must be stressed, at this point, that we do not necessarily have to accept the perspective and interpretations of these women as containing some kind of objective truth. In any case, I am sure that readers with a university connection will wish to question any view that, by remaining within a university environment, they fail to maintain significant contact with external issues and concerns - either professionally or personally. What is seen to be important is that the construction of the university world which emerges from the experiences of these able and determined women leads them to a view that the intrinsic benefits of their experience only come to fruition when taken away and applied elsewhere. That such a view is substantially affected by minority status in a masculine world cannot be in doubt. But in saying this, it also needs to be stressed that the women's view is not a rationalisation of any incapacity to enter the university world of graduate research. It is much more the case that the university is simply seen as another institution for the promotion of learning, but that once significant levels have been reached, the locus for the utilisation of all that has been learned - and this is much more than mere academic knowledge, skills and understanding - has to move outside the confines of the academic world.

In this respect, therefore, it can be suggested that, by allowing these students a chance to explore and articulate the results of self-reflection, we are in a position to use their views to show that universities, by emphasising their detachedness, conceivably create the conditions for their own rejection by a significant group of intelligent students. It is tempting to speculate that the 'new' universities, with their open fields policies of building outside their host towns and cities, and emphasising a self-contained campus design, have, in fact, created environments which are counter-productive to the achievement of any kind of useful synthesis between the worlds of academe and society.

In saying this, we do not mean to suggest that universities should change their ideological commitment from that of detached academic enquiry to one of engaged political action - though some would clearly argue this. It is, however, to suggest that were those in positions of power to examine more carefully the impressions they and their institutions create upon their students, they might begin to wonder whether the message they were seen as transmitting was exactly the one they would intend. The potential gulf between the hidden curriculum of university experience, as perceived by one particular group of students, and the manifest intention to promote expertise and understanding by inducting students into continuing that tradition, has been highlighted in this examination of the views of women physics students. The existence of such a gulf should be intensely worrying. It is also important to try to determine the extent to which it exists within the perceptions of students other than the small minority we have considered in this chapter. There are indications, as we shall see in Chapter 7, that this gulf exists within the experience of all the groups of students we have considered. It is too easy to dismiss its existence as simply showing that students will always have a tendency to misinterpret what is set before them.

Being a Woman Physics Student

   The implications of the perspectives of the women students contain one last, important point. By denying themselves the opportunity to enter the world of university research, they fail to produce, in the long term, a nucleus of women academics in physics. In consequence, the continuation of a male preserve, with its own implications for the image of physics which is perpetuated, will be unabated. Whilst their entry into the industrial world will bring some parallel improvements, the lack of substantial careers guidance in schools is likely to inhibit future generations from knowing this. Their determination not to enter teaching further ensures that the teaching of physics, at almost all specialist levels, will remain predominantly a masculine preserve. There is no need to search for any kind of conspiracy theory to see that the result of women physics students developing the perspectives we have outlined, can only serve to ensure that the university sector will play a substantial part in the continuing role of education as a contributor to social differentiation.

Chapter 7

THE STUDENT EXPERIENCE

A number of factors, with varied kinds of significance, emerge in each of the preceding chapters. This chapter will draw together those which appear to have a bearing on the nature of the higher education experience of students. It will be important to begin, though, with an examination of the issue of generalisability in the Introduction.

It might be helpful to tackle this issue initially by pulling together the conclusions which emerged out of the preceding five chapters. The first reported on what might clearly be taken as a general situation faced by the vast majority of students, and experienced within every university - that of the arrival in a strange place and a new institution of a large number of first year students. Clearly there will be a variation of circumstances - large and small cities, central and peripheral university sites, old established and much younger universities, separation of teaching and residence or their integration, different patterns of departmental and faculty structure. Nonetheless, a common feature for the students will be that of strangeness - they are unlikely to know many other people, they are away from their own familiar circumstances, for many of them this will be their first experience of independence, and they will be surrounded by staff and other students who are already familiar with the routines and customs of the place.

Initiation and integration, and the problems which beset students in making sense of this new world, are universal. What could indicate the peculiar nature of the report on experiences at York is the substantial evidence of the dysfunction between the intentions of those responsible for making the induction of new students easy and those same students' perceptions of the difficulties of under-

The Student Experience

standing created by the arrangements made to help them. What seems to be important here is the evidence that only through contact with the incoming students is it possible to see that most of them seem to be more confused than helped by university, departmental and student arrangements designed to be of assistance. To rely on the views of those responsible for making the arrangements - the official perspective - would support the idea that everything is being done which could be done, and that all anticipated problems have been catered for.

What matters, from the students' point of view, is not that people should be seen trying to be helpful, but that any assistance should be beneficial. It seems to follow, therefore, that those in positions of responsibility need to take measures to become aware of the attitudes, expectations and feelings of students if they are to be able to focus their energies on what matters to the students. It is obviously not enough to take an administrator's view on what <u>should</u> be a problem for students. We can argue, therefore, that the evidence from this initial study does have relevance beyond York to all universities. This relevance rests on the need for awareness of the student perspective whenever decisions are being made which are designed to affect and influence student attitudes. This is not to say that the student initial experience in all universities is identical with that described at York. It is, however, to stress that the official perspective on student views could significantly misrepresent those views.

The possibility for gaps to widen between staff and student perspective must be large for two main reasons: one is that students are transient, and generationally separate from the majority of faculty; the other is the obverse of this and rests on the fact that faculty are relatively much more permanent. The overall result of these circumstances is likely to be that while new generations of students continue to reflect their age group's changing cultural values, faculty will continue to refine a traditional perspective. The only source for significant change within this latter perspective must be the recognition of changing circumstances which are seen to require modification of some kind of the traditional assumptions. Such changes could result from changing external pressure sources, e.g. recent changes in government policies about the funding of universities producing modifications of traditional views about autonomy. Alternatively, changes can be seen, historically, to have come about through the development of fresh institutions. Thus the expansion of civic universities around the turn of the century brought substantial change in the variety of courses being offered, in the modes of entry to courses, in the kinds of students for whom a university education became a realisable possibility, in the expansion of the number of staff responsible for decision making in the increased numbers of universities.

Similar developments can be seen throughout the 1960's with the 'new' universities pre- and post-Robbins. Many of these have pioneered novel arrangements of course structure, patterns of government, student-staff relationships, by concentating on what have been percieved to be the merits of aspects of institutions in which the new faculty gained their qualifications and early experience, With the reversal of expansionist policies in recent years the opportunities for such innovation must decrease - if not completely vanish. Additionally, the lack of opportunities for the appointment of new staff - always a potential source of fresh ideas - is unlikely to inhibit further the consideration of new approaches. It is clear, too, that the publication of the discussion document (D.E.S. 1978), drawing attention to the possible implications of the declining school population for universities, was also a source of significant thinking about desirable modifications to course structures, entry qualifications and the extent of university provision.

Without such internal and external stimuli to consider alternatives to current practice, it would not be suprising to find that facultyu members, with a concaern for the furtherance of knowledge in their own fields, will be likely to continue to maintain their current practices in organising courses for their undergraduate students. In doing a so, it is also likely that they will find that the experiential evidence which this produces could, from their perspective serve only to reinforce their views that present practices are at least satisfactory. By puttingan emphasis on the academic side of the university experience, the staff perspective fits coherently within an an academic commitment to research and understanding. In its narrowest manifestation, this would even deny the relevance of any information emerging from consideration of the student perspective, From this pointof view, the neophyte cannot be conceived of as having anything signifi-

The Student Experience

cant to offer even over matters of direct concern.
We can take the examination of the staff-student gulf a stage further by reassessing the implications of Newell's examination of student study habits within the History Department. This has a number of fresh elements to add to the complexity of the analysis. There is, in the beginning, an extended examination of the nature of the traditional perspective which operates within the library and which is reinforced through professional associations and reflections on established practice. This tradition rests on an assumption about the foolish student who is unable, through lack of proper training, to make use of the extensive resources which a library contains. The traditional answer to this problem, modified over time, by the incorporation of new media of communication, has always been that of more and better guidance on how to make the best use of a library. Behind this approach lies an assumption that the nature of student learning - and specifically this is concerned with undergraduate learning, although it can be seen to have implications for graduate study as well - is similar to that of the experienced researcher.

Detailed examination of student learning practices and extensive discussion with course tutors responsible for the formal contexts within which this learning occurred, showed that a very different situation prevailed. What figured most prominently for these students was their perception of the requirements of the course and, from that point, the determination of the most effective strategies for the finding and using of appropriate library resources. The staff perspective is determined by a recognition that students are not experts in the particular field of study and that, in consequence, they are best helped by some systematised guidance into the variety of library materials which might have a bearing on furthering their understanding. The outcome of this approach is, not at all uncommonly, to provide a very carefully organised book-list moving from essential reading through to highly specialised material perhaps relevant to tiny aspects of the overall theme. An indication that many of the works cited themselves contain further reading, with pointers within the text to indicate their centrality, is also sometimes given.

It does not require detailed guidance on the use of a library if the only function it serves is to house already identified material. Nor does it require much more than ordinary common-sense to divine that, whatever cataloguing system is in operation, books on the same shelf as those already identified are also likely to contain material on the same themes. The problem of understanding student study habits thus changes from a concern with how to help them make more effective and original use of a library to one which now raises the problem of a conflict between the ideology of academic staff and the results of their pedagogic practices.

One aspect of this conflict is what Newell described as 'time-management', i.e. that students are subject to a number of competing demands on their time - not all of which are academic - and which are impossible to meet in their entirety. Their own inclinations and expectations will figure largely in the way in which they determine priorities for action. To complicate this problem further is the evidence of the interpretation of the 'hidden curriculum' with which students appear to operate. This interpretation seems critically to contain the view that learning history is predominantly the acquisition of bodies of knowledge; that staff, through their reading lists and suggestions, are giving a clear indication of the limits of the required knowledge.

The consequence of these factors operating together is to provide a situation which fits neatly into the typology offered by Entwistle and Wilson (1977) of syllabus-bound and syllabus-free students. The complication here, though, is the fact that whilst many students would like to feel they were able to operate in such a way as to incorporate material resulting from their own researches, their perception of the pressures upon them is such as to make them feel they do not have the opportunities to engage in such original approaches.

It is conceivable that it is the very few who manage their time in order to be able to inject their own interests into the officially prescribed reading are the ones who show signs of becoming 'real' historians. The majority will simply be satisfied with getting degrees. Given that the History Department attracts a very large number of highly qualified applicants each year - last year there were nearly 1700 applicants for a quota entry of 100 places, and the average A level performance of those admitted was 3 B grades - the potential for greater development is clearly present. That

The Student Experience

it does not get realised to the extent to which it would appear possible, seems to result from staff practices confirming a student perspective which is at odds with the ideology within the department. The references to international experience by Newell, together with the confirmation of findings at York within the different circumstances of a neighbouring university, would seem to confirm the universality of this experience. If this experience is as widespread as a number of studies indicate, then it must be important to recognise that the learning process - as it is conducted, as well as how it ought to be conducted - should be considered as important as the organisation and structure of the content of academic courses. Without such an attempt to get out of the students themselves the parameters which define and, in the majority of cases unfortunately limit, the learning potential of their study habits, it would be unlikely that staff concerns themselves would bring such features to light.

In fact Newell's chapter itself suggests that the nature of the staff reactions to students' performances would be much more likely to see the shortfall in achievements as the result of specific inabilities in the students than the natural outcome of the pressures within which the students have to live and work.

Rothschild confirms this problem - of balancing social and academic pressures in her study of 'mature' students, i.e. those who had interrupted the normal process of coming to university directly from school. The context section of Chapter 1 has already indicated that York has a relatively small proportion of such students - only 79 students aged 21 or over who were admitted to undergraduate courses in 1981 out of a total entry of 986 students.

Before exploring some of the issues which emerged from this study, it is worth noting that, as with Newell, the author started the enquiry with a firmly-held belief, based on her reflections on her own experience of a 'year-off'. This belief was, essentially, that no-one should be allowed to enter higher education without "a year's pause for consideration of life outside the walls of academe". The first part of the enquiry thus became a predetermined quantitative investigation designed to uncover the benefits of 'time out'.

What emerged from this stage were two main points: one which identified significant differences between those students who had only taken one year off and those for whom the interruption in their education covered a substantial period of years. The other identified those taking one year off as being relatively undifferentiated from students who had come to university direct from school. This lack of differentiation related to the fact that both groups appeared to follow a pattern dictated by what the majority of their friends had done. Thus, if friends came straight to university, the tendency was for others to do the same; but if friends took a year off, this, therefore, while representing a different decision from the normal, seemed to represent no more active a decision, nor yet one which predicated a different view or expectation of higher education.

Following up this preliminary approach by depth interviews with 'mature' students produced other kinds of information, much of which could not have been anticipated and which was, in many cases, counter to the anticipated expectations based on the author's own views. We take these findings as casting further doubt on the value of the normative tradition of educational enquiry - the quantitative, hypothesis-testing, controlled approach. Two points are at issue here: if we are to be concerned to unravel the working perspectives of students as they react to their experiences of university life, we must be very sure that we are aware of the significant parameters if we are to design the traditional psychometric research approach. The evidence of our studies, together with other similar interpretive reports, indicates that much that might be taken for granted within the official perspective on students - the perspective within which academic researchers reside - bears little relationship to what is actually the case. It follows that, by building a research tradition on the results of approaches which are themselves questionable, we are highly likely to compound the errors in our understanding.

By presenting the outcomes of studies designed to allow students to speak for themselves, we hope to contribute to a greater understanding. From this point of view, returning to the substance of Rothschild's study, it can be seen that the staff perspective on breaking the continuity of the educational process between school and university contains at least two elements which do not appear to relate to the experiences of the students concerned. Firstly there is the clear focus of concern solely upon the implications for academic performance -

The Student Experience

whether this was science staff feeling that, because of the nature of their subjects, any break would be to the detriment of academic progress; or whether it was arts staff who could determine no difference in academic functioning among the different kinds of student. The other element was concerned with the identification of an apparent lack of concern with social and affective dimensions of the decision to take a break.

Given the earlier results concerning the complex interaction between social/affective and academic/cognitive pressures within which students are faced with making many important decisions, the above results become more than interesting. This added dimension becomes more critical in the light of developments within the University during the current academic year.

Two committees - the Teaching Workshop Committee, with a brief to help staff to consider problems they themselves identify, and also to help to induct new staff into the University; the Committee for Continuing Education, with a brief to explore ways in which the University can extend its opportunities beyond the normal range of degree courses - had combined to suggest that there was some concern across departments about problems faced by mature students. To examine these issues three things were done. An open seminar was held with invitations to anyone interested in the problems to attend. Out of this a further workshop was held to which outside speakers were invited and for which a survey was also undertaken across the University's population of mature students.

As the first seminar progressed it became clear that what had started as a clear understanding of the peculiar problems of mature students became modified towards a concern for a range of difficulties which all students might experience. Amongst comments made were those which hinted that it may be that mature students were more noticeable in relation to these problems - and were consequently identified with them - largely because they took the trouble to explore their difficulties with tutors to a greater extent than did the normal undergraduates.

A comment made in the later enquiry by a mature student emphasises the above point: "As a mature student I feel I was more aware of my difficulties, and was able to assess my weaknesses and discuss them with my supervisor". From this point of view it is also worth adding a comment made in the summary of this enquiry: "The specific measures suggested would mostly be of advantage not just to mature students but to all students irrespective of age". An additional point was also made out of this enquiry which focused attention on a highly-specific aspect of the situation of some mature students - those who are married and/or have children. Here the concern was with residential facilities and the worry created by being faced with an even greater problem of finding suitable accommodation as compared with single students.

The focus of discussion in the final seminar - led by Dr. J. Wankowski, who has made many notable contributions to the study of the student experience - reflected the emergence of the perspective, already noted, that all students have problems. From such a standpoint, it became important to notice the emphasis on the range of circumstances surrounding student difficulty and the lack of much formal consideration given, within academic planning to these factors. While there may be attempts to cater for serious problems which do emerge - through varieties of counselling services - it is difficult to find much evidence of approaches based on prevention.

To this extent, therefore, we can take this additional source of information as reaffirming the earlier contention that the faculty perspective is essentially dominated by a concern for academic/cognitive levels of performance, and does not appear to take into account the other dimensions of the real world within which students live and work.

Returning to Rothschild, with this new background, some other emergent features take on greater significance. The greater degree of involvement in student activities of mature students for example, indicates perhaps an enhanced capacity to cope with the competing demands. Alternatively, it could indicate an interest in using the university experience in ways which are wider than the merely academic. In this sense, mature students can be seen as reinforcing the original finding that, as a result of their time out, they were able to see the opportunity of higher education as an end in itself. In this they were certainly different from the normal students who, predominantly, saw the university experience as a means to an end.

Most noticeable, though, was the evidence from the series of interviews of the eventual blurring of distinction between mature and other students. While the mature students may have settled in more quickly than the others, from the second term onwards, in terms of worries, nervousness and pressure, very little real difference could be discerned.

To conclude the examination of mature students it is worth adding some summary information from the questionnaire report conducted for the Teaching Workshop seminars. The survey was conducted across a random sample of the 275 mature undergraduates in the University and, in the first part of the survey, they were asked to comment on aspects of any differences between themselves and other undergraduates. The results are given in the following table:

Table 7.1 Mature students' perceptions of differences from other undergraduates

Factors	Differences Yes	Perceived No
Motivation	32	12
Basic Skills	11	32
Oral Skills	30	12
Use of Sources	14	29
Memory	16	27
Establish Relationships with Staff or Students	21	24
Integration in Departmental Life	19	26

Notes: The figures above represent numbers of respondents. The 'Yes' column conflates replies in which a positive indication was given, but which was further divided into categories representing greater or lesser.

From the table, it can be seen that only two factors stand out, from the mature students' point of view - Motivation and Oral Skills. In this respect, in spite of the substantially different method used, there is some connection with Rothschild's findings. It would appear that the attitudes and expectations of mature students do differ markedly from those students who come to university straight from school. Both their maturity, as well as their clearer understanding of their purpose in being at university, could reflect their feeling that their oral performances - in seminars and tutorials - are better than those of other students.

If this difference in oral performance actually does emerge - and is not the result of a false perception - within small group teaching contexts, it would be surprising if staff were not to notice mature students easily. If, in addition, the other evidence of their concern to explore their difficulties with staff rather than hide them is also correct, such a combination could readily lead to mature students being perceived of as having more problems in coping with academic life than ordinary students. Again, therefore, we have the possibility of misinterpretation of evidence resulting from a faculty allegiance to a view of students which is narrowly conceived.

Gillie's brief study of the problem of overseas students further emphasises this aspect of the situation. It incidentally, and sometimes explicitly, also calls into question a number of assumptions which appear to be entailed in official views of overseas students. In times when differential fees are being charged to overseas students, it is important to ensure that a clear, unambiguous definition of who counts as being such a student is used. That the situation continues to be confused is highly likely in the situation created by the Nationality Act (1981). When the consequences for students identified as being from overseas are as financially damaging as the present situation of charging full cost fees involves, the individual is very much at risk. It will be interesting to see how the government decided to overcome the difficulties presented by the House of Lords' judgement.

The most important feature to emerge from Gillie's interviews - both in their conduct and in their content - was the problem of language, and that students from America found this as much as did those for whom no form of English was a first language. Not only did the students feel that this was a major problem for them, they also felt that indigenous students and staff did not recognise the magnitude of the problem. In this respect, it is of interest to note that Gillie, in practising before conducting the interviews, found a similar example of this in the contrast between her own North East accent and that of a fellow London student.

What is interesting about the problem of language is that the difficulties it was perceived as creating were far less to do with academic situations than with social relationships. These latter difficulties were reflected both on the campus as well as in terms of making wider use of the opportunity of living in a foreign country. Weather, dress, language, all had to be adjusted to, but things

The Student Experience

that in this country we would take for granted became double problems. If customs and practices are strange, and if languge seems more a barrier to communication than an aid, it is difficult to see how many of these problems can be readily overcome. If, at the same time, the initial problem of integration into a strange new university community is even greater, it is not surprising to find that overseas students react like any other students; that is, that they seek out people in similar circumstances to their own and gain confidence through reducing their isolation. The consequence is obvious: overseas students are forced into the company of other overseas students and thus exaggerate the problem of lack of contact with the majority indigenous student population.

In trying to break down this barrier, the lack of social language makes for even greater difficulty. What is much more likely to be the result of English students sticking together for similar reasons of lack of confidence, is then perceived as being representative of an expected aloofness and lack of interest. It seems that it is a feature of the student experience to find groups of like-minded others - whether through social or academic contacts - and, eventually, become more inward than outward looking. Perhaps the recognition of the essentially transient nature of the university experience for students enhances this development. A campus university, organised on the principles involved in York's design, can offer greater opportunities for wider social mixing beyond narrow departmental or faculty boundaries. Nonetheless, the consequences would, in principle, appear to be more the result of any situation of entry into a new environment than peculiar to a single institution. If the picture of ordinary students so far presented can be seen as typical of any institution, there are no grounds for feeling that the situation of overseas students presented is also other than typical.

The only major difference which might result from the special features of York rests in the relative smallness of the number of overseas students on the campus. This situation, too, could be compounded by the lack of significant residents within the city from other than British backgrounds. In other words, the degree of isolation felt by overseas students at York could be much greater than that experienced by overseas students in universities with larger overseas contingents or sited in conurbations with larger numbers of overseas residents.

The Student Experience

An advantage could, however, result in York's overseas students being forced to be much more cosmopolitan in their social contacts than might otherwise be the case. It might be seen as something of a pity, though, and to the disadvantage of the majority indigenous student population, that the international nature of the overseas students' social groups tends not to include students from the host country.

The last point to be stressed here from this study again reflects the major concern underlying this book: the evidence of the gulf between the student experience and the staff perception. In the case of the overseas students this was seen by the students also in relation to language problems. From their perspective, they did not feel significantly disadvantaged in academic discourse. On the whole, they felt they could follow lectures, and participate in seminars and cope with written demands in English. Their command of the functional and limited language of academic discourse was not, for them, a major problem. They were, however, of the opinion that staff felt that they had a problem in following and meeting the academic requirements of their courses.

Given the earlier evidence concerning the inter-relationship between the academic and social dimensions of the student world, it might not be surprising that a group of students, who experience a substantial range of problems of adjustment to a strange set of social circumstances, also experience some academic difficulties. If English is not their first language, and if the main focus of the staff perspective is a concern for academic performance, then, conceivably, academic difficulties can easily be seen to stem from language problems. A symptom of the difficulty of social integration becomes transmuted into a cause of academic difficulties.

The final study, by Lewis, of women's experiences within the Physics Department, confirms two views which have arisen in the previous reports: the existence of a clear student perspective which reflects the complexity of the world in which they have to cope with significant academic demands, and an indication that, without a knowledge grounded in a direct awareness of this student perspective, it is unlikely that non-students would recognise the salient features which constrain the student experience.

The reflection of similar findings in another detailed enquiry in London would appear to indicate

The Student Experience

that the results are not peculiar to York. In the same way, the constant references in each of the studies to equivalent findings emerging from similar studies in other institutions, also gives credibility to the universality of the features observed in these studies in York. In spite of the kinds of differences alluded to in Chapter 1, which clearly differentiate a variety of aspects of the organisational and administrative arrangements at York, it would appear that the context does not seriously affect the processes which impinge upon and influence the student experience.

The opportunities for greater staff interaction with students, which was a hall-mark of the initial planning, and which was intended to develop an integral community identity, do not seem to have produced the desired results. While there may be greater opportunities for contact than in some other universities, even if these opportunities are taken, there does not appear to be much evidence of the impact of increased staff knowledge of student perspectives which should have emerged. Where evidence of staff perspectives has been brought to light in a number of these studies, it serves only to confirm a view, established in a very different context by Becker et al (1968), that the faculty perspective does not incorporate an awareness of the "socially structured conditions of student performance," (p. 131).

Each group with whom we have been concerned - incoming students, history students, mature students, overseas students, women physics students - can be seen to have a number of features in common to their varied experiences. They each live in a complex world in which personal/social demands compete with academic/formal pressures. Each student has to be able to cope with this complex array of forces and, to be successful, has to operate in terms of personally-determined priorities. In deriving these priorities, it seems that the 'hidden curriculum' of the university plays a significant part. This 'hidden curriculum' consists of the assumptions which are perceived by students to exist within the formal, academic aspects of their world. Whether the students are correct in their assumptions, or not it is clear that they are strongly influenced by what they believe to be the faculty perspective as reflected in the 'hidden curriculum'.

If the student view is correct, then the faculty perspective would appear to be at fault, by offering conflicting messages. On the one hand, what is desired; on the other, what is practised. In this respect, we see a situation little different from the kinds of conflicts which Beard (1968) outlined. If the student view is incorrect, the problem becomes one of communication to ensure that the message received is the one which the faculty intend to be transmitted. In either case, because of their permanent and institutional positions, the onus must lie with faculty to ensure that the situation is remedied. One feature of any remediation must surely lie in greater staff-student co-operation, since misunderstanding, or a lack of understanding, can only continue if both parties rest in ignorance of each other's positions and expectations.

From the staff point of view, it seems clear, from our results, that one critical area is the lack of appreciation of how the personal/social world of the student influences the way in which the formal/academic world is perceived. The continued existence, at the social level, of relatively isolated sub-groups of students, further shows how the impact of the academic dimension of the University reinforces the initial circumstances of differentiation. Thus, incoming students tend to stick together initially, to minimise their lack of confidence, and to share their inexperience. Mature students also stick together, because they settle in more quickly, have a clearer sense of the use to which they wish to put their university opportunities, and make wider use of the range of extra-academic resources available to them in the University and in the city. Science and arts students operate under different time-table constraints and, as a result, tend to mix less with each other, and also make differential use of the other than academic sides of academic life. Overseas students, also feeling strange, find indigenous new students unwelcoming, and are also forced to socialise amongst themselves. Women physics students, recognising the predominant masculine attitudes and assumptions which permeate their world, see the University as an institution in which only 'lads' are likely to feel permanently at home. In spite of their relatively high abilities they persist in seeing their future as lying outside the University context in what they persist in calling the 'real' world.

In almost every case, the image that each separate group presents, to faculty and to other students, results in a false conception of critical aspects of that group. This is nowhere better demonstrated than in the chapters dealing with mature students and history student. In each case, the behaviour of the students is wrongly interpreted to fit with assumptions which do not match the ways in which the students themselves describe their circumstances. The result, for faculty and for students, is that the same behaviour gives rise to different interpretations and these, in their turn, are taken to reinforce the perspectives out of which the interpretations emerged. The lack of significant staff-student contact, outside the confines of the academic curriculum, ensures that this cycle of misinterpretation is complete and self-sustaining. In the same way, although to a lesser degree of significance, the separate student groups continue to preserve, by and large, their separate identities - thereby failing to recognise that they each share more in common than any superficial differences in their perspectives of each other would indicate.

If this kind of outcome can occur, and be as widespread as to be found in each of our separate enquiries, in a university like York, it must at least be possible that it exists to an even greater extent in universities built upon different principles. The existence of similar findings in other studies which have also focused on an examination of student perspective, suggests that the gulf between staff and students' views is endemic to the present state of university education. We conclude this chapter, therefore, with a brief discussion of why this might be so, and why more traditional approaches to research in higher education have failed to highlight this major problem.

It is of some direct relevance to note that, in the context of a conference devoted to examining the evidence from the past fifteen years of experience of higher education, and using this to explore potential future developments, the various papers in Oxtoby's (1981) collection continue to give greatest priority to the academic perspective. McAlease (1979), already quoted in Chapter 1, has indicated that the educational technology approach prevailed over that concerned with effective training for university teaching in the reception of Hale (1964) and Brynmor Jones (1965) reports. To this extent, therefore, one major message of the climate of university expansion, post-Robbins, has been to confirm the primacy of the academic perspective grounded in a limited concern for matters directly pertaining to academic courses and attitudes.

There is, it is true, an indication that other factors than those of motivation and ability can influence student learning, as Entwistle's (1981) opening paper in this collection shows. However, the message from his review of much research into student learning is still that much of it is concerned to focus on the technical side of things; a focus which is further narrowed in terms of the psychometric paradigm adopted in the majority of the studies quoted. However, as Entwistle also notes, "much current research is correcting the excessively psychological emphasis of the earlier research by recognising the effects of the learning environments or contexts on how students learn and on their study strategies," (p. 19).

It is very much to be hoped that the collection of studies reported here is seen as yet another contribution to this developing perspective. Such a desire is manifest in terms both of the content which such student-centred studies produces, as well as in terms of correcting the excessively quantitative orientation of the research tradition in higher education.

If the results of research in higher education are to be of benefit - or at least of interest - to faculty and administrators, whose concerns are not directly with issues to do with effective learning, then one of the benefits must result from increasing awareness of the assumptions which are taken for granted within the faculty tradition. Quantitative approaches and controlled psychometric designs - as Entwistle and Wilson (1977) pointed out - are unlikely to perform this function. This is because the nature of the research design within which they operate must predetermine the nature of the enquiries made of students and of staff. Without a detailed critical examination of the nature of what constitutes the perspective of these two separate groups, it is difficult to see how appropriate questions can be formulated. In consequence, the results which emerge from such studies will serve only to reinforce the perspectives from which the original formulations were made.

A summary of the studies reported here must therefore suggest that the information which has emerged - both from students and, very importantly, in most cases mediated by people who were themselves students - does indicate a range of circumstances peculiar to the student experience and which the traditional faculty perspective does not take into account. As Kewlock (1975), an undergraduate

The Student Experience

reflecting sensitively and critically on his university experience, put it: "the university is thus never getting around to its real aim - to foster the development of certain aspects of the student's personality and outlook ... It examines only a superficial representation of knowledge that does not reflect these qualities," (p. 91).
From this point of view, it should have been unnecessary for universities to be concerned with 1990's problems of a new kind of clientele - see the Discussion Document, D.E.S. (1978) - in order to identify a need to consider possible developments of different kinds of course arrangement, or different kinds of staff responsibility. In the same way, it should not have required a concern within the University of York for the perceivedly different problems of mature students, to identify a need to understand the complex nature of the undergraduate experience. Whatever the extent of faculty commitment to their own research interests, and the consequent reinforcement of assumptions embedded in the practices of their discipline, such a specialised focus should not exclude an awareness that the majority of students are unlikely to have strongly academic vocational intentions.
It is on the basis of a consideration of the factors which have been identified as influencing the student reaction to the academic demands which faculty make, that the final chapter will be concerned to explore the implications of the education aspect of higher education. By showing that, for students, a wider view of the educational implications of their higher education experience is prevalent, we feel that this provides a novel basis for examining this question. In doing so, we shall, of course, make reference to a variety of other sources. The stimulus, however, comes from the co-ordination of the findings of our own studies. It is because each one of these has been seen to reflect and expand the issues identified in the earlier ones, that we feel it important to use this added insight into the student world as a foundation for examining ways in which the benefits of that experience can be enhanced. By making this information available to a wider audience, we hope that its implications will spread beyond the single campus in which it originated. Because, too, any consideration of implications will reflect the set of values and assumptions of those making them, it is also clear that there can be no unique solution. While we go on to offer our own views in the next

145

section, it is clearly important to recognise both that others may very well disagree with our formulations, and also that they are perfectly entitled to draw their own, different conclusions. That both will incorporate reflection on the student experience is enough.

We started this section with a two-fold purpose: to pull together what were seen to be the significant findings to emerge from each of the preceding reports; and to explore the question of their uniqueness or otherwise in relation to their university of origin. Any reader may, of course, wish to argue over the extent to which other aspects than those identified above are of greater significance. What has been taken as the main indicator of significance here is anything which leads to the clarification and elaboration of the nature of the student perspective on the university experience.

In doing this, we feel that the strong evidence of the conflicting pressures between the academic and social dimensions of the student world are common to each of the studies outlined. In addition, the studies are seen to complement and overlap with each other in terms of the features of the student world they uncover. The further point to emerge concerns the student view - either explicitly or implicitly - of the faculty perspective which seems, from the students' point of vantage, to be much narrower in focus.

Within a university expressly designed to promote a community identity between staff and students, and which also puts a premium on small group teaching, it is disconcerting to find such a consensus of evidence. From the organisation and structure of the University of York, as already outlined, there must be strong support for the view that the situation in many other universities might not even be as rosy. Those features of the student world which have been identified do not appear to be peculiar to the university in which the studies took place; rather do they appear to be dimensions of the normal student experience. Where administrative or architectural features do not contain the same potential for staff-student relationships as those at York, the only differences which might be expected lie in terms of the gulf between student and faculty being even wider than those identified here. The implication must be that even well-intentioned staff - and surely this should be the vast majority - will be misconceived in their attempts to offer solutions to their stu-

The Student Experience

dents' problems. By concentrating on the academic or technical dimensions of the student world, faculty miss both the evidence of the social world which students inhabit as well as the impact which this social world has on any student's capacity to react satisfactorily to academic demands.

As long as a lack of knowledge of the detail and the complexity of the student experience is characteristic of the faculty viewpoint, so long will organisational change - or its absence - fail to reflect the full possibility inherent in the experience of higher education. To say this is not to be dismissive of the present values of the university experience. Students still increase the demand for places each year. Nor, however, do we take the evidence of the student perspective to suggest the irrelevance of the traditional faculty view. Instead we wish to argue that, if the University is to become a true community, then all parties involved need to become more fully aware of all the factors and pressures which affect their respective circumstances. By stressing the student perspective we hope we have, in a small way, added to other attempts to rectify the present imbalance of understanding.

Students need to become aware of the critical factors which appear to them to indicate the dimension of the hidden curriculum which staff impose, in addition to understanding the overt details of their course demands. On the basis of our evidence, students seem to be very effective in understanding the faculty view. Because it is the staff of a university who are clearly in positions of authority and therefore capable of implementing changes, and who also, on our evidence, fail to appreciate the full and complex nature of the student world, we hope this contribution will both aid their understanding and also stimulate consideration of the implications. Our own assessment of the consequences follows in the next section.

Chapter 8

THE CONSEQUENCES FOR HIGHER EDUCATION

It is important to define the agenda for this chapter, both to make explicit what it will contain, as well as to indicate areas of deliberate omission. There must always be a danger, in any case study based on a single institution, of assuming too much by way of generalisation to all comparable institutions. There is also the danger to be guarded against of being over-enthusiastic for naive solutions to complex problems. Finally, while seeing student concerns as having a high priority, we shall try to limit discussion only to those areas of university development where relevance can clearly be demonstrated. This last point means that we shall say nothing about other important matters, like university finance and administration, nor shall we be overly concerned with distinctions between the public (polytechnic) and private (university) sector of higher education.

For convenience, we shall divide this last chapter into four separate and self-contained sections. In the first, we shall examine the immediate consequences of the picture of the student experience we have presented; in the second, we shall explore some of the implications for approaches to more effective student education; in the third, we shall discuss the implications for research into higher education; and the final section will raise some general questions about future developments in higher education. It should be noted, in passing, that each section will be presented with the commitment outlined in Chapter 1 very firmly in mind: that the intended audience is the general university community rather than that highly-specialised sub-group of educational researchers. References to other works in this chapter are intended, therefore, to serve a functional purpose rather than the typical,

Consequences for Higher Education

symbolic role of indicating the extent of the author's reading and ideological commitment together with an indication that the work makes universal connections.
   The aim is, and must be, limited. Limited only to those issues which the author sees arising from reflections on the findings presented and the connections with other, demonstrably related work, Limited also in suggesting that readers are much better placed to examine their own institutions for comparisions and contrasts with what might appear to be relevant in one particular university. Limited, finally, in stressing processes rather than products as the most useful way forward to the many complex questions surrounding the future definitions of the term 'education' in the description of the 'higher education' sector of the British education system.
   However, it should also be noted that, by stressing the limitations of this chapter, we do not also intend to undervalue the evidence we have presented. Nor do we wish to suggest that the implications of this evidence are unimportant. The limitations simply serve to recognise that too much should not, without other supporting evidence, be built on modest foundations. They are, effectively, a recognition, on the part of the author, of the constraints which need to govern the contents of the following sections. As with other interpretations which have been offered in the course of this book, it will be for the reader to check that the bounds of these constraints have not been overstepped.

Immediate Consequences
   Entwistle (1981), quoting Carter's presidential address to the 1971 annual conference of the Society for Research into Higher Education, noted that "Perhaps the main purpose of research on student learning should be seen as raising the 'level of awareness' of both staff and students by describing as fully and clearly as possible the ways in which students try to cope with the tasks and situations they meet in higher education. This may leave us merely describing Carter's quaint and awful things. Can this process of description also help to make things better?" (p. 32).
   Entwistle concluded by suggesting that "general prescriptions either for staff or students are unlikely to be uniformly effective. The ideas emerging from the research have to be reinterpreted

by each individual within the unique context of his own aims, ideals, knowledge and skills. No general formula should be expected to more than provoke this individual re-examination of personal relevance and meaning," (ibid. p.33).

We take these quotations - coming as they do from the concluding section of a survey of the field of studies concerning students and student learning - as indicating a stress on a process outcome from our enquiries as being more relevant than attempting to provide a panacea. The one significant result to which we drew attention in the last chapter concerned the self-fulfilling way in which student perceptions provide academic staff with evidence of student performance. The ways in which staff react to their estimation of this performance provides the students with further cues which reinforce the original perspectives even further. To break out of such a cycle requires awareness on the part of those involved that their perceptions might misrepresent the evidence at their disposal. It also indicates that any solutions to the problem must lie with the participants. This must be the case on two counts: one that, if awareness grows, the possibility for changing reactions must exist and the relationship between the participants could also change; the other that, because individual perceptions play such a great part in determining the interpretations put on behavioural evidence, it is difficult to see them being amenable to rational argument or persuasion. Foster, Ysseldyke and Reese (1975), in another context, but dealing with a similar issue, summarised this state of mind in the title 'I wouldn't have seen it if I hadn't believed it'.

One way of beginning to break out of the spiral of self-defeating perceptions would be for those involved with student initiation, mature students, overseas students, student resources, and all the other sub-groups into which the student population can be variously divided, to start to reflect upon the assumptions they hold and which underpin their actions. For example, to what extent do we conspire to make it difficult for new students to <u>become</u> students by contributing to the growth of the 'freshers' week' industry? To what extent are the various events, arrangements and opportunities - all organised with the best of intentions - serving other ends than those of the incoming students? To what extent, by serving to accentuate the strangeness of the situations in which new students find

Consequences for Higher Education

themselves, do we provide a context which reinforces sub-group identity and inhibits the early development of a university-wide community?

Similar questions can be asked in respect of each of the particular sub-groups which we have explored in earlier chapters. Because there is evidence from other university contexts - both in this country and abroad - that a central problem is the different perspectives with which faculty and students operate, we can generalise with some confidence to all other student sub-groups and to all other higher education institutions. This somewhat sweeping assertion is bolstered, however, by reference to a range of studies of which only a few examples need be offered here. Merton et al (1957) and Becker et al (1961) both provide evidence from American medical contexts showing how the hidden curriculum of courses comes to shape the views of intern students and, further, how the resulting student performance is taken to mean somewhat different things to the faculty. Becker et al (1968), in their Kansas study, effectively showed, on one American campus, that this situation seems endemic to the university-wide situation of students and results in the same mis-match of interpretations of the same behaviour by both faculty and students.

In this country, those concerned with student counselling services - and who therefore come most frequently into contact with student problems of many kinds - all draw attention to the ways in which students can misconceive academic expectations and, in doing so, provide evidence which staff take as justifying the earlier judgements. Raaheim and Wankowski (1981), drawing on experience in Birmingham and Norway, identify this problem very clearly, as does Wright (1982) in her description of findings based on her work at Reading.

Other research studies in this country, exemplified by Entwistle and Wilson (1977) in their national sample survey, Miller and Parlett (1974) in their Edinburgh study, Percy and Salter (1976) and Ramsden (1979) developing similar studies in Lancaster, and Gibbs (1981) drawing on experience and research at the Open University, all point to the same conclusion. There would, therefore, appear to be sufficient evidence, from a wide range of soruces, to suggest the respective and misconceived assumptions which lie behind the perceptions of both staff and students provide the key to the problem of more effective student learning. The detailed findings of our own parochial enquiries fit neatly into these other results and add yet further weight to these conclusions.

It follows from this that the onus for breaking the spiral of confusion must rest with the faculty staff. It is their messages which are being misconstrued, and it is they who provide evaluative judgements which, when mediated to the students, are taken to reinforce the prior misconceptions.

If we now recall some of the sources of misconception to which we have drawn attention, it will be possible to provide additional pointers to ways in which staff might begin to contemplate ensuring that the messages they really want to transmit are the ones which are eventually received.

By emphasising the complexity of student life and experience - via university authorities, departmental meetings, student union activities, society publicity - a range of people, with the best of intentions, provide two stumbling blocks which make the transition to being a student unnecessarily difficult. Firstly, they reinforce the natural apprehension of the incoming students by detailing the difficulties of, say, time and money management, and the more complicated study skills required by work at the university level. This gives substance to ill-articulated fears about the complications yet to be faced, and appear to force the incoming students back on each other for support. Thus, instead of seeing senior university figures as potential guides and mentors, they are immediately cast in the image of successful initiates, models of people who have successfully negotiated the pitfalls they have described in graphic detail. New students are left to look for guidance from those least capable of offering it - themselves. The cycle of segregation has begun.

Segregation becomes further refined in relation to other identifiable sub-groups of students. In our case, these have been seen as mature students and overseas students, with some indication of lack of contact between science and arts students as well. While the mature students appear to have fewer problems about immediate initiation - sensibly seeming to take little interest in most of the 'fresher' activity, and being very concerned to become students immediately, overseas students, on the other hand, are forced to highlight their student role, because of the difficulties which appear to inhibit their easy socialisation with indigenous students because their command of English falls short of easy social discourse. In both cases

Consequences for Higher Education

there is evidence that these sub-groups are seen, by many academic staff, as experiencing peculiar problems of learning which distinguish them from the majority of 'ordinary' students who have come straight from school. In the one case, because mature students recognise difficulties which they face and are sufficiently confident to be prepared to broach these with staff - thereby providing staff with evidence that they experience more, and sometimes different, problems from those of the 'normal' student. In the other case, the social diffidence of overseas students in learning contexts - resulting from their lack of integration into the main student body - and their reticence in engaging fully in discussion, are taken to indicate a poor command of English which could affect their capacity to follow their course effectively.

Women physics students appeared to be picking up other messages of a more subtle and complex kind, but the consequences have many similarities with the situations of the other groups. They are relatively isolated from the majority of their fellow-students as a result of the social and cultural values through which both groups have grown up. In addition to this, they do not see the university community as one in which it would be profitable for them to contemplate making a future - even when they are clearly capable of continuing with research studies. The university world, whether rightly or wrongly, is perceived by them as unreal, not grown up, and therefore not a suitable place in which to put their knowledge and skills to further use.

Finally, in terms of study habits - particularly with respect to using libraries - we found evidence of the distance between staff and students reflected in the student perceptions of staff as authorities, both of their subject specialisms and also of the grading of student work. The immediate consequence was that, in spite of staff intentions to provide opportunities for students to begin to do small-scale original and independent work, students operated predominantly within the guidelines they took from preliminary booklists. By demonstrating a lack of originality and independence they confirm the faculty perspective that students are not really capable of such activities.

Effective Student Learning
In this section we shall examine three issues which bear on how it might be possible to ensure

Consequences for Higher Education

that the learning of students can be enhanced, so that they can optimise the benefits available to them from their experiences of higher education. The consequences of the previous section will be followed by an examination of recent attempts to derive principles for more effective curriculum development. This, in its turn, will lead to a brief consideration of the problems of defining student learning.

One major concern must be, as indicated above, to break the self-fulfilling cycle of misinterpretation. Heightened awareness of the difficulties in a two-way relationship is, in principle, the responsibility of both parties - staff and students. However, in an institution characterised by a significant hierarchical structure, it must surely be the responsibility of the more powerful to make the first moves to improve the situation of the least powerful groups. Consequently, it has to be accepted that the onus rests with academic staff to make the first moves in any reconsideration of how to improve student learning. We shall examine, later in this section, some of the weaknesses of what appear to be the traditional responses to such exhortations - curriculum reforms, modifications to assessment requirements, the introduction of relevance into courses. Initially, we must be concerned with the implications of the total context within which students are expected to meet academic demands.

Unless academic staff can take into their consciousness the fact that students live in a complex social world in which academic demands form only one part, it is difficult to conceive of how significant changes in approach can come about. An immediate requirement therefore must be that academic staff take pains to find out about the dimensions of the world which students inhabit, the pressures they feel, the competing demands made of them. This cannot be done by relying solely upon a contrived mechanism of supervision, with institutional procedures and relatively sparse contact. Percy (1983) has commented that "Students' unions, college, medical, careers and counselling services more frequently point to ambiguities in the teaching aims, lack of information, unrealistic assessment deadlines and so on, as well as personal, domestic and financial circumstances of individuals as contributing to student learning difficulties," (p. 96).

He makes the contrast between this description of some of the features of the student world and the relatively brief labels which are characteristics of academic discussion of students. "It is not uncommon for lecturers to label students as "weak", "lazy", "plodding", "bright", etc. and to leave it at that", (ibid). The implication of such a contrast is that the faculty perspective is narrow, being bounded by the tight constraints of a concern solely for manifest academic performance. Such a view appears to take no cognisance of the complex context within which such academic performances must be mediated. It is to mistake the evidence of one dimension as representing the reality of a multidimensional universe. Such a narrow commitment to academic indicators may, in fact, be wholly consistent with the situation of the professional university teacher, committed to research and enquiry within a disciplinary area. In which case, the problem of getting academic staff to accept the need to take into consideration more than a student's academic work becomes a problem requiring a substantial change in orientation. Such problems are parallel to those of the Catholic Church in terms of the difficulties experienced in accommodating Galileo's conclusions about the solar system - they require the rejection of a set of assumptions which have previously been more than adequate, and their replacement by a new model of the world.

While the gap continues to exist between staff and students - and it clearly does even in a university like York with its design and principles to encourage informal contact - it is difficult to see how evidence will be alternatively interpreted. For the gap to be closed, it is not necessary that staff attempt to pass themselves off as students, nor would it be necessary for academic staff to deny their cultural habits. What is required is that staff make attempts to use the opportunities which are naturally available to try to understand the nature of the student world. This must involve greater communication between staff and students as well as a reconsideration of the actions and behaviours which are currently the norm of academic life.

If this means that more thought needs to be given to individual and collective contributions to undergraduate courses, that must be for the better. To stop at that, though, or to see the solution as resting solely upon removing the kinds of global inconsistency in course design to which Beard (1968) called attention is to misread the need. It is necessary, of course, that inconsistencies in course

Consequences for Higher Education

design are eradicated. It is unfortunate - as any consideration of many university courses still shows - that course content and aims and assessment requirements can still be seen to be in conflict with each other. In addition, as Miller and Parlett (1974) showed, such conflict is further complicated by the various perceptions which different students have of the academic game they are involved in playing.

It is also a pity that, from a student's point of view, a variety of course components can still be organised in such a way as to require a single date for the submission of a range of work for assessment purposes. The pressures which this creates - and not at all resolved by the kinds of trite statement that careful management of time is all that is required to resolve the issue - force the student into making priorities, seeing each work requirement as in competition with the rest. Course requirements thus become barriers to synthesis and broader understanding.

One of the staff respondents to the official enquiry into mature students referred to in Chapter 4 made an important point which bears directly on this question. Using evidence from a department dealing with a large number of mature students, the response included the following :

> Nearly all the written material on how mature people learn assumes that the process is merely an extrapolation from what we know of childhood learning - Piaget and all that. It isn't. What material there is assumes that learning is chiefly a matter of memory. We think that skill-learning and attitude-learning follow different patterns from rote-learning - and different patterns from each other.
> From our observations we think that the learning processes of adults may best be explicable in Gestalt terms.

It is of more than passing interest to see the formality of reference in the above quotation to a particular approach to psychology. Most commentators are agreed that the notion of a Gestalt refers to a holistic appreciation of a system in a way which cannot be achieved by the alternative consideration of its separate parts. To this extent, therefore, it can be seen to be analogous to the eventual overall view which most academic departments wish

Consequences for Higher Education

their students to achieve on completion of the total programme. A view of history becomes more than the understanding of particular periods, and the fuller understanding of any particular historical event is enhanced by a global concern. Similarly, in science, as Kuhn (1970) has argued, the contemporary student can only be said to be a scientist through the "sort of learning (that) is not acquired by exclusively verbal means. Rather, it comes as one is given words together with concrete examples of how they function in use: nature and words are learned together. To borrow once more Michael Polanyi's useful phrase, what results from this process is "tacit knowledge" which is learned by doing science rather than by acquiring rules for doing it", (p. 191).

If it is the case that all university courses - save, perhaps, the purely vocational ones, and even that caveat must be questionable - do imply the eventual achievement of some kind of holistic understanding of the nature of the discipline then, at the trivial level, it must be important to ensure that the administrative arrangements within the course do not create barriers to the achievement of this end. At the more complex level, it is incumbent on the lecturers to ensure that their own practices, in dealing with students, are also consonant with this aim.

The corollary of this is that approaches to curriculum development in higher education will be misconceived if they take, as underlying principles, allegiance to some notion or other of a developmental kind. To do so would be to fall into two major errors. One in dealing with a curriculum which becomes a reified entity and unconnected with the real world in which it is expected to be implemented. We can refer to this as the Schools Council error, since it exemplifies the ineffective approach to curriculum reform throughout the 1960s and 1970s which that body was noted for. The other error results from attempting to deploy a theory of learning which would seem to be inappropriate when applied to learning within higher education - where every student must, almost by definition, be seen as having reached the required end of adult level performance.

Wilson (1981) provides perhaps the most extensive and most recent example of a large-scale approach to the problem of curriculum reform in higher education and which seems to fit the approach just outlined. While recognising the influence of peer group pressures, the importance of student perceptions, the key influence of the image which staff provide, Wilson nonetheless draws the conclusion that what is required is a context of learning which will allow for and encourage an orderly development "from a relatively passive conception of their role as learners at entry ... to role conceptions which are more active, thoughtful, questioning and challenging, and which reflect growth in confidence in themselves as learners", (p. 163). Eventually, Wilson completes his review by arguing "that the curriculum and its assessment are the key factors affecting the quality of student learning," (p. 172).

The aims identified in the first of the above quotations are laudable, and provide a suitable encapsulation of the essential aims of undergraduate courses. The problem lies in a conceptualisation of an ideal process towards the achievement of these aims which appears to lose sight of the social context within which such development is expected to take place. It also fails to take into account what Lewis and Vulliamy (1978) and Shattock and Walker (1977) found in relation to the varied aims and expectations which students have of their period of higher education.

Unless staff can move to a situation in which inroads into student perceptions can be made, even the best of curriculum models will be doomed to failure. Without students gaining experience, through direct contact, of what it is like to operate in an "active, thoughtful, questioning and challenging" manner, most of them will never achieve this desirable end. And this will not be because they are incapable of doing so. It will be the direct result of the pressures to which they are subject in their complex world, compounded by the images of staff which these pressures result in them acquiring. Mere exhortation to adopt an alternative model will not be enough - that, too, can be misinterpreted. Co-operative experience, with staff exemplifying the experience and the practices they wish their students to adopt, must be one of the major ways in which such changes can begin to come about.

Leftwich (1981) has explored in some detail one significant strategy for the implementation of such changes. In advocating the adoption of case-study, problem-solving approaches to undergraduate learning, though, he takes a very different stance from many who support such proposals. Part of his

Consequences for Higher Education

argument rests on the relatively incontrovertible case that, if we want students to develop such capacities as "'the general powers of mind', 'critical ability', 'thinking for oneself', 'insight', 'self-education', 'judgement' and so forth" (p.40), we should adopt pedagogic practices which are appropriate for the achievement of these ends. It follows that we should not remain wedded to traditional patterns of learning - via lectures, seminars and tutorials which are tutor and curriculum bound - which demonstrably produce "superficiality of thought, the re-cycling of standard ideas or fashionable orthodoxies, a fragmentation of understanding through disciplinary monism, and - above all - an incapacity to cope with the de facto inter-disciplinarity of a difficult world and its complex problems" (p.41).

However, a significant feature of Leftwich's argument - which fits with the conclusions we have already drawn - is the recognition that "such pedagogic re-structuring would have far-reaching implications for the current arrangements and ideology of teaching in the universities," (p. 51). Amongst the areas in which consequent change is necessary, Leftwich indicates the need for long-term departmental planning, active participation in decision-making by staff, a substantial change in the traditional division of labour within departments, the growth of inter-disciplinary contacts, changing assessment practices and assumptions, the development of co-operative staff-student learning relationships, information exchanges, staff training. He concludes by arguing that "The academic profession is the single most serious obstacle in the way of pedagogic innovation in the universities", (p.56). The reason for this lies in the perceived needs of academic staff to remain wedded to the traditional relations of teaching and learning "because most current arrangements provide considerable time and opportunity for getting on with consultancy work, or non-teaching-related research and writing on which, crucially, promotion or advancement within the profession demands," (p. 58).

We make no apologies for dwelling at length on this particular argument, simply because it represents one of the very few attempts to recognise the political and social context of the university world within which any proposals for change must be promulgated. Without such considerations, it is likely that rational arguments, based on theoretical principles, will continue to be a recipe for non-consideration within the world of academic staff. Consideration of the real world which academics inhabit leads to a recognition that they, too, have perceptions which affect their view and that these perceptions are all too likely to embrace assumptions which, as Leftwich has indicated, make them singularly unreceptive to emphasis on the teaching aspect of their jobs.

The interests of the academic staff, in present circumstances, are singularly incompatible with those of the students for whose learning and education they are responsible. A major consequence of this conclusion is that there would appear to be only two possible ways forward if the learning and educational experience of students are to be enhanced; if universities are to offer learning opportunities which stand a reasonable chance of altering present traditions. We exclude, here, the ever-available prospects of individuals being able to make significant changes within a limited course area.

Of the two possible ways forward, only one seems politically credible, and that relates to the need to enter some kind of moral crusade, an emotional rather than a rational call for action. Such a moral argument would be based on the selfishness inherent in the academic perspective which, by emphasising the needs of research and publication, undervalues a commitment to undergraduates. If academic attitudes and commitments are as deeply entrenched as Leftwich avers, then, like all such attitudes, they will be unamenable to rational persuasion. On this ground alone it is difficult to see as realistic the possibility that whole departments, let alone whole universities, will change their orientation towards their courses, and put a premium on enhanced student education. Evidence that this will improve the quality of learning will not be sufficient inducement to change to those wedded to a perspective which sees little relative value in a commitment to student learning. Equally unrealistic, certainly in the foreseeable future, is any source of external influence which, through control over finances, would be likely to exert pressure for change in traditional teaching practices in universities.

By taking into account the political, social and institutional dimensions of student learning, we have been led to recognise the salience of these dimensions in the formation of the traditional academic perspective. The nature of this perspective,

Consequences for Higher Education

and its incompatibility with that of the students, leads to the conclusion that the enhancement of student learning on any large scale will only result from a change in academic attitudes. Such a change is only likely to emerge if academics can be persuaded of the immorality of their relative lack of professional concern for the students for whom they have a formal responsibility. To exercise that responsibility will require the recognition of the extra-academic dimensions of the students' world.

Research in Higher Education
In this section, we shall concentrate on only three aspects of another large area of concern: the orientation of much research into higher education, the lack of significant contact between research and traditional academic interests, and the parallels which can be drawn between this situation and that of research into the school sector of education.

The emphasis in the continuing series of Leverhulme seminars on aspects of higher education is a nice example of the global concerns which exercise many people when they consider questions about this sector of education. To say this is not to minimise the importance of such concerns, and it would be absurd in present circumstances for significant attention not to be given to financing, patterns of government, inter-sector co-operation, and alternative possibilities in which, for example, not all universities would be treated as equivalent institutions. Mere self-interest, if nothing else, would serve to justify such an agenda. However, such questions are also intrinsically important to the nature of higher education, and from that point of view also needs discussion. it is, though, of some significance to note that in the report of one of the recent Leverhulme seminars - cf. Wagner (1982) - which focused attention on institutional change, only the editor's introduction - based on reflection on the other contributions - makes an attempt to be concerned with the context of learning which such changes might induce. Even this introduction spends most of its length in exploring strategies for change at the national and institutional level. There is one brief mention of a need for peer-group evaluation of courses, and an indication that, amongst other benefits which might accrue from this development, "it might raise the status of teaching in universities," (ibid, p.20). It is as if consideration of important questions requires the adoption of a perspective which only recognises the significance of national and institutional features, and fails to take into account the small-scale, personal implications.

Such a description would also appear to be true of much research into higher education. As Wilson (1981) has pointed out: "The psychometric tradition has exerted a powerful influence on the study of student learning," (p. 20). This tradition can be recognised by a number of significant hallmarks which Elliott (1978) has categorised as including: its scientific perspective, using definitive concepts, requiring quantitative data, leading to the statement of formal theory, based on experimental methods and formal generalisations, drawing on external observations using a priori categories of classification.

Correlational studies, based on quantitative data collected on the basis of a limited and predetermined set of categories in which a relationship is presumed, leaving only its strength to be determined by the enquiry, are frequently to be found within this tradition. In the context of curriculum change and evaluation in schools, Parlett and Hamilton (1971) have scathingly criticised this tradition as representing the transition of an 'agricultural-botany' tradition into the human area of education. Given a large-scale, sample survey kind of approach to educational questions - which even at a common-sense level, let alone in terms of any serious consideration of methodological issues, involves personal relationships and a commitment to organic processes - it is not surprising to find Entwistle (1981) concluding "that the impact of educational research on both policy and practice, perhaps in most areas of research and decision-making, is indirect," (p. 2).

What is perhaps more questionable is whether, as Elliott (op.cit.) has argued for school-focused studies, research in this quantitative, psychometric tradition can conceivably be considered as educational. It is not educational simply because, almost by definition, it transcends and redefines the real world of education in order that it can be treated in an objective and quasi-scientific fashion. The need for operational definitions within the psychometric tradition means that the language used to describe the real world of the participants being researched has to be translated into concepts which make them largely unintelligible to those they purport to describe.

A modification to our earlier assertion, in the

Consequences for Higher Education

previous section, that there are only two major ways forward when contemplating significant changes to make student learning more effective, can now be made. This would require the proliferation of such studies as we have reported, and which are based on attempting to operate within the common-sense world of the groups whose perspectives we have attempted to discern and describe. As Ramsden (1981) has argued, on the basis of reflection on a series of similar studies in Lancaster. "Specific suggestions for changes to teaching and learning must wait until detailed case studies of individual departments have been carried out," (p. 66).

While disagreeing with the imperative in the above comment, it is possible to agree with the need for the encouragement of an alternative to the traditional model of research into higher education. An alternative, moreover, which would give some semblance of credibility to the motives, dispositions, intentions and perceptions of those who are actively engaged in the process of learning. It is conceivable, if also optimistic, that a proliferation of evidence which reflects the complex reality of the world of universities, and which is recognisable by academics and students, could assist in the development of favourable attitudes towards teaching and learning.

Journals are, however, beginning to carry increasing numbers of articles reflecting a shift in the thrust of research into higher education. It is because such journals are not the major item in academic reading, because of the orientation towards academic development in their own particular specialisms, that a strategy of gradual change, resulting from an increased awareness of evidence which bears directly on teaching, is not likely to be an effective initiator of major changes.

The situation in respect of higher education is, in many ways, reminiscent of the early 1970s when Young (1971) heralded the arrival of a new approach to the study of schools. In his critique of traditional approaches to research on schooling, Young made a number of points. These included the fact that many researchers were content to take as problems issues defined for them by those in positions of power and influence in education - teachers, administrators and politicians. From their points of view, a concern for organisational arrangements, a concern for standards of measured educational performance, a concern for the pathology of the failures, or a concern for new curricula designed

Consequences for Higher Education

to meet changing official demands on schools, were realistic. What Young went on to point out was that many of the concepts used in such enquiries "must be conceived of as socially constructed, with some in a position to impose their constructions or meanings on others," (p.2). Bernstein (1971), in a contribution to Young's collection, argued that because of this commitment to official definitions and problems, "the sociology of education has been reduced to a series of input-output problems; the school has been transformed into a complex organisation or people-processing institution; the study of socialization has been trivialized," (p.47).

As was mentioned in Chapter 1, it is possible to acquire a large amount of information about the input-output dimensions of the university world. The DES, and UCCA and the UGC, all produce detailed annual statistical accounts of qualifications of students and eventual destinations, together with substantial information on finances of the university sector. Others, like Trow and Halsey (1971), for example, have produced detailed results of enquiries of a statistically descriptive kind, of the nature of academic staff. Studies of student drop-out abound. Explorations of alternative sources of financing both students and universities exist within literature, but scarcely any of these could be said to reflect the ecology of the university world. Miller and Parlett (1974) argued a case for "an 'ecological' metaphor for research into educational processes on the grounds that the circumstances must be studied as well as the issues of substantive concern which exist within those circumstances," (p.114).

An ecological approach, by definition, demonstrates its recognition of the reality of the experiences of those researched. A whole array of publications, since the advent of Young's (1971) collection, have shown that a concern for the processes and interactions which characterise the real nature of education in schools can deepen our understanding of the complex mechanisms which are involved, and open our eyes to factors of significance which generations of traditional quantitative studies had failed to highlight.

A further dimension of developments within the school sector of education in recent years is also worthy of note in this connection. This reflects an increasing understanding, on the part of those involved with in-service training of teachers, of the need to change the orientation of their courses from being product centred to being committed to

Consequences for Higher Education

working with teachers on approaches to teachers' problems. Out of such developments has come further support for encouraging teachers to engage actively in research into aspects of their own institutional practices and assumptions.

If there is a significant job for educational researchers in higher education, then it must lie in developing good co-operate working relationships with their other academic colleagues; to enquire with them rather than into them; to show that educational research can be directly concerned with problems which academics recognise. Only by working with their academic colleagues, in exploring the nature of their problems, is it at all likely that researchers will begin to get recognition for the critical role of taken for granted assumptions underlying the problematic nature of these given problems. As we have seen earlier in this chapter, it is academic perspectives which are the key to unlocking the potential for enhanced learning which is buried within the present traditions of university teaching.

Increasing numbers of teachers are becoming aware of the benefits of a concern for the processes of education, and the competing nature of the perspectives of students and teachers within those processes, as a result of alternative approaches within the sociology of education in recent years. Similarly, more teachers are being inducted into a realisation that they should not rely on outside researchers to provide evidence which bears on their immediate concerns. If such changes can be brought about within the much larger domain of school-based education, subject as it is to the greater vicissitudes of public concern and visibility, then there must be some optimism about the possibility of similar changes taking place within the university sector as well.

However, it is clear from the evidence at the school level, that such changes can only come about if there is a significant switch in research emphases away from traditional, large-scale, quantitative enquiries and towards novel, small-scale qualitative and interpretive approaches. If, at the same time, these approaches can offer the additional prospect of co-operation between academics and professional researchers, the chances of increased and heightened awareness by academics of some of the significant features of the ecology of universities is substantially enhanced. An awareness of these ecological features, which will naturally vary from one univers-

Consequences for Higher Education

ity habitat to another, can then also be brought to bear on the other important questions concerning universities at their institutional and national levels.

Our plea, in this section, for a substantial alteration in the balance of the research enterprise in higher education must not, therefore, be taken as indicating a lack of recognition of the importance of other, large-scale questions. Nor should it be taken to indicate an opposition to quantitative studies. It should, however, be taken as being based on the straightforward assumption that student learning is affected by the way in which academic influence is perceived in a complex social and personal context, by students. This result is now well-established in a number of studies as well as in our own researches at York. It follows that further contributions to the study of the processes through which both student and staff perspectives are reinforced through their mutual experiences of teaching and learning, can only serve to expand our understanding of this obviously complex area further. Such understanding, we suggest, is unlikely to emerge from enquiries based on the large-scale quantitative tradition - which is best left, therefore, for the study of those questions to which it is demonstrably suited. In addition, we would argue, the large-scale enquiries, which might be needed to provide evidence on institutional-sized questions, would also benefit from being able to relate their relatively impersonal analyses to the more personal insights derived from small-scale interpretive studies.

Future Developments in Higher Education

A large part of this final section will be necessarily speculative. Other parts will stress imperatives for action which are seen to arise from our work so far. We see no problem in recognising these points at the outset. They result from two separate approaches to the current situation within universities. One is the lack of precision with which any substantial forecasting can be entertained about the universities. The university world has still not completed the policy changes forced upon it by changes in government policy. This, amongst other things, had led to a revision of the consensus of the past twenty years since the Robbins Report, that there should be places available within higher education for all those qualified to benefit from such courses.

Consequences for Higher Education

Not only has that significant change taken place, but it emerged essentially when the beginnings of policy outlines were crystallising out of discussion of the 1978 D.E.S. Discussion Document about the universities in the 1990s. This document, it will be recalled, indicated a future in which a greater degree of openness might become a reasonable possibility as universities were faced with coping with their additional accommodation - built to cope with the major post-war birth-rate bulge - and a substantially reduced 'normal' prospective population. The possibility that changes in age-participation rates may also emerge as a result in changing perceptions of a rapidly altering employment market, as well as consequent upon changing patterns of government financing, has also been raised (D.E.S., 1980).

It can be argued, for example, that, if there is to be a diminishing market of potential applicants for undergraduate places in the future - for whatever reasons - this could force universities to be more amenable to contemplate changes to ensure that they attract sufficient members to justify their staffing and other expenditure. One of the ways in which this might be done is to offer courses and patterns of teaching which are demonstrably attractive to potential students. The Times Higher Educational Supplement (30 September 1983) called attention, in a third leader, to the need for academic to recognise the changes in the public conception of higher education - from a general good to a consumer product - in their reaction to popular summary descriptions of different universities. A cursory examination of advertisements for polytechnics and colleges of higher education in the daily press shows that the public sector of higher education is already aware of the need to sell its courses to potential customers.

However, the likelihood of market forces playing a significant part in bringing about heightened academic awareness of the need to be more concerned with students is moderated somewhat by the contrary indications of government considerations for alternative funding principles. These, if press reports are true, could have the opposite effect and greatly reduce the numbers of prospective students, and the size of universities, so that no change in market forces comes about. Or, in some forecasts, the change acts in the opposite direction by making it even more difficult for students to gain entry to the courses which remain available.

Consequences for Higher Education

In such a case, the need for universities and their academic staff to change their habits and assumptions is eradicated.

Our findings, supported by those of, for example, Macdonald (1977), Ward (1977), Percy and Salter (1976) and Shattock and Walker (1977) - and recently supplemented by the views of Wright (1982) - is that today's students have wider expectations of higher education than a narrow commitment to the 'pursuit of excellence'. We have no grounds for believing that this is a novel situation, and personal reflection would indicate that similar expectations go back at least a generation. One key feature of these wider student expectations - and one which usually comes to light in student reflections on dissatisfaction with their actual experiences - is a commitment to personal development and a more general education that they can find both interesting and relevant. It is these expectations which, in a previous section of this chapter, in elaborating on the arguments of Leftwich, we argued were the explicit aims of universities, but aims which the practices and priorities of academics inhibited from their fullest realisation for the majority of students. Lewis and Vulliamy (1978) examined this aspect of the student experience for students taking combined degrees in great detail, and confirmed the findings of the Nuffield Study Group in their larger enquiry.

It does not, therefore, require a concern for any future changes in the nature of potential university student populations, to suggest that there should, today, be a concern within universities that such aims are not being realised. Paradoxically, there are small signs that one of the unforeseen consequences of the recent changes in the financial positions of many universities is beginning to force academics into consideration of ways of modifying their teaching practices in ways which might make the learning of students more nearly achieve the intended aim. The lack of traditional levels of support for staffing and library resources, for example, are already beginning to have an effect on course planning, teaching relationships and assessment practices, and many of these changes will result in closer staff-student co-operation in learning. It is surely odd to find that reductions in economic resources could produce a situation in which the traditional aims of universities are more likely to be achieved than has seemed possible during the more palmy days of substantial post-

Consequence for Higher Education

Robbins expansion. Perhaps academic freedom, completely unconstrained, can lead to licence and irresponsibility, where personal interests take precedence over commitment to students?

The move to modular courses - which the Nuffield Study Group has earlier indicated as a significant trend in course planning in higher education - is another solution which is seen as a way of coping with the foreseeable dilution of resources. As Mansell (1977) has pointed out, one consequence of such developments is that they require close staff co-operation and consultation, together with the development of effective procedures for student counselling. Again we come up against the institutional barriers to institutional innovation which Leftwich has so extensively analysed. Some consolation, though, can be taken from the fact that, if developments take place on any large scale, it is most likely that co-operation, consultation and counselling will emerge - because, otherwise, the scale of the problems faced will be too great.

A further worrying trend can be seen in the current emphasis on university courses demonstrating a greater degree of vocational relevance. This, together with the increasing, and, according to the J.M.B. (1983), misleading, reliance on ever-increasing A level grades to control and restrict entry to a diminishing university sector, can only lead to a narrowing of the overt aims of university courses. This, if it takes place, will demonstrably serve only to increase the disaffection and alienation of new generations of students who, if they are anything like their predecessors, really want the traditional aims of a broad and general education within a disciplinary context.

However, as Lewis and Vulliamy (1981) argued, when we reflect on the dimensions of student expectations "This spectrum embraces at least the following elements: vocational concerns, academic interests, personal education, a concern with wider social issues, a need to reflect and mature before entering the world of work. Those universities which do not recognise these needs in planning their courses will, through the 1980s, increasingly find that they are unable to attract sufficient numbers of even traditionally motivated school leavers to retain their viability," (p. 179).

A specific sector of the potential university population is represented by the female half of society. It would be doubly unfortunate if, in reacting to current pressures, universities were seen to be implementing policies which reduced the possibilities for women in higher education even further. The contraction in teacher training from the mid 1970s has already reduced substantially a set of opportunities which women frequently took up. The continuing lack of academic opportunities within the university sector for successful women graduates will only serve to make the situation for women students even worse than the picture we have presented in Chapter 6. If women students currently see the university world as an enclosed and inward-looking men's club, and one whose features are decidedly unattractive to them, the recent report on male domination of the academic profession (E.O.C., 1982) will be followed by even more disquieting reports in future.

We can point, here, to the notion of detachment as one of the major elements which women physics students found unattractive, and made them wish to seek employment and research opportunities outside the university world. This detachment undoubtedly fits with a traditional academic faculty perspective of an objective and timeless pursuit of truth. Given that the vast majority of students will always wish to leave their universities on completion of the degree courses, the implications of this state of affairs add yet another dimension to our consideration. It is a further indication of the nature of the source of the gulf between the faculty and the student perspectives to which Becker et al (1968) originally drew attention.

Tenure, however, and a commitment to academic freedom should carry with them a recognition of academic responsibility for providing the most satisfying environment within which the majority of university populations - students - though transitory, can be enriched. To say this is to echo the need for a moral dimension to the argument for supporting change in university patterns of teaching, and in staff and student relationships in learning, which has already been discussed.

The further element for consideration and incorporation into official thinking in universities, as they grapple with the uncertainties of future government policies, needs to be the encouragement of small-scale research within individual universities. For too long have most academic sociologists and educationists been concerned with exploring other sectors of education than their own. It is time that pressure was put upon them, within their own institutions, to turn their gaze inwards and

Consequences for Higher Education

attempt the process of demystifying their own practices. It is, and must remain, a serious criticism of higher education that its academic members are very ready to turn their critical faculties on almost any aspect of the known and unknown world except their own doorsteps. Without the assistance of these colleagues, who have demonstrated their expertise with respect to schools, it would be absurd to recommend that other academics should change the habits of a lifetime, and engage in enquiries for which they have neither the general inclination nor the expertise.

To fail to recognise the reality of the student situation is to be culpable of failing to recognise and accept the complete set of responsibilities which society has every right to expect of members of university faculties. To put off consideration of alternatives to present practices until the anticipated 'new' students of the 1990s emerge, is likely only to exaggerate the problems which university staff will then have to face. If universities wish to generate a climate in which they are seen as socially valuable institutions, and justify the relatively high costs of their existence compared with the other sectors of education - through which, incidentally, the majority of the population pass - one major way forward can only be through concerted staff consideration of ways to improve the present learning experiences for the students for whom they are currently responsible. There is a significant role for educationists and sociologists within universities to play, in co-operating with their academic colleagues in helping, in the first instance, to describe the reality of the learning relationships between the staff and student bodies.

If this co-operative enterprise can be taken further in all universities, as we have shown it can be done in one, then the future, for both staff and students, when compared with today's experience, will only be describable as a world of difference.

REFERENCES

Barzun, J. (1968) The American University, Oxford: Oxford University Press
Beard, R.M. (1968) Teaching and Learning in Higher Education, Harmondsworth: Penguin
Beatty, L. (1977) Students' Needs in relation to the Library. Report of work in progress at The Institute for Educational Technology (unpublished), Guildford: University of Surrey
Becker, H.S., Geer, B., Hughes, E.C. and Strauss, A.L. (1961) Boys in White, Chicago: University of Chicago Press
Becker, H.S., Geer, B. and Hughes, E.C. (1968) Making the Grade, New York: Wiley
Bernstein, B. (1970) A Critique of the Concept of 'Compensatory Education' in Rubenstein, D. and Stoneman, C. (eds.)
Bernstein, B. (1971) On the classification and framing of educational knowledge. In Young, M.F.D. (ed.)
Bierstedt, R. (1957) The Social Order, New York: McGraw Hill
Blackie, J. and Gowenlock, B. (1964) First Year at University. Revision of Truscott, B., London: Faber and Faber
Blackstone, T. (1976) The education of girls today. In Mitchell, J. and Oakley, A. (eds.)
Blishen, E. (1983) Donkey Work, London: Hamish Hamilton
Brewer, J.G. and Hills, P.J. (1976) Evaluation of reader education. In Libri, 26, 1, 55-62
Brynmor Jones Report (1965) Audio-visual Aids in Higher Scientific Education, London: H.M.S.O.
Byrne, E.M. (1978) Women and Education, London: Tavistock Publications
Carey, R.J.P. (1968) Library instructions in colleges and universities of Britain. In

References

    Library Association Record, 7, 66-70. Quoted in Scrivener, J.E. (1972)
Cicourel, A. (1964) Method and Measurement in Sociology, New York: Free Press
Currie, J. and Leggett, T. (1965) New Commonwealth Students in Britain, London: Allen and Unwin
Deem, R. (1978) Women and Schooling, London: Routledge and Kegan Paul
Department of Education and Science (1978) Higher Education into the 1990s: A Discussion Document, London: H.M.S.O.
Department of Education and Science (1981) Annual Report 1980, London: H.M.S.O.
Department of Education and Science (1983) Annual Report, 1982, London: H.M.S.O.
Douglas, L.E. (1964) Types of Students and their Outlook on University Education: A Comparative Study of Students in the Physical and Social Sciences. Unpublished Ph.D. thesis, London: London School of Economics
Driver, C. (1971) The Exploding University, London: Hodder and Stoughton
Dyson, A.G. (1975) Organising undergraduate library instruction: the English and American experience. In Journal of Academic Librarianship, 1, 1, 8-13
Ebbutt, D. (1981) Girls' science: boys' science revisited. In Kelly, A. (ed.)
Elliott, J. (1978) Classroom Research: Science or Commonsense? In McAleese, R, and Hamilton, D. (eds.)
Entwistle, N.J. (1981) Students and Student Learning. In Oxtoby, R. (ed.)
Entwistle, N.J. and Percy, K.A. (1974) Critical thinking or conformity? An investigation of the aims and outcomes of higher education. In Flood Page, C. and Gibson, J. (eds.)
Entwistle, N.J. and Wilson, J.D. (1977) Degrees of Excellence: the Academic Achievement Game. London: Hodder and Stoughton, Educational
Equal Opportunities Commission (1982) Sixth Annual Report 1981, London: H.M.S.O.
Flood Page, C. and Gibson, J. (eds.) (1974) Research into higher education, 1973: papers presented at the sixth annual conference of the Society in December 1973. London: Society for Research into Higher Education
Foster, G.G., Ysseldyke, J.E. and Reese, J.H. (1975) I wouldn't have seen it if I hadn't believed it. In Exceptional Children, April, 469-473
Gibbs, G. (1981) Teaching Students to Learn - A

References

    Student-centred Approach, Milton Keynes: Open University Press
Hale Report (1964) Report of the Committee on University Teaching Methods, under the Chairmanship of Sir Edward Hale, London: H.M.S.O.
Halsey, A.H., Heath, A.F. and Ridge, J.M. (1980) Origins and Distinctions, Oxford: Clarendon Press
Hammersley, M. and Woods, P, (eds.) (1976) The Process of Schooling: A Sociological Reader, London: Routledge and Kegan Paul
Harding, H. (1983) Switched Off: The Science Education of Girls, York: Longman for Schools' Council
Head, J. (1980) A model to link personality characteristics to a preference for Science. In European Journal of Science Education, 3, 295-300
Head, J. (1981) Personality and the learning of mathematics. In Educational Studies in Mathematics, 12, 339-350
Heap, B. (1982) Choosing a Degree Course, Richmond: Careers Consultants
Holbech, B.A. (1967) Transition: A Personal Crisis. In the Times Educational Supplement, 7th July
Iliffe, A.M. (1969) Are sixth-formers old enough for university? In the Times Educational Supplement, 11th July
Joint Matriculation Board (1983) Problems of the GCE Advanced Level grading scheme, Manchester: J.M.B.
Kelly, A. (ed.) (1981a) The Missing Half: Girls and Science Education, Manchester: Manchester University Press
Kelly, A. (1981b) Girls and Science Education: is there a problem? In Kelly, A. (ed.)
Keylock, B. (1975) A week in the life ... of a university undergraduate. In Higher Education Bulletin, 3, 2, 86-92
Kuhn, T. (1962) The Structure of Scientific Revolutions, Chicago: University of Chicago Press, 2nd ed.
Leftwich, A. (1981) The Politics of Case Study: problems of innovation in university education. In Higher Education Review, 13, 2, 38-64
Lewis, I, (1983) Some issues arising from an examination of women's experience of university physics. In European Journal of Science Education, 5. 2. 185-193
Lewis, I, and Vulliamy, J.G. (1978) I heard it through the grapevine, York: Department of

References

    Education, University of York
Lewis, I. and Vulliamy, J.G. (1981) Student Perspectives in Higher Education: some implications for future university planning. In Educational Review, 33, 3, 171-180
Library Association Record (1949) 51, 149-150. Quoted in Scrivener, J.E,, 1972
Macdonald, K.M. (1977) University Selection and Educational Culture. In Higher Education Review, 9, 2, 58-68
McAleese, R. (1979) Staff Development in higher education, 1961-78, Part I. In British Journal of Teacher Education, 5, 1, 107-132
McAleese, R. and Hamilton, D. (eds.) (1978) Understanding Classroom Life, Windsor: N.F.E.R.
Merton, R.K., Reader, G.G. and Kendall, P.L. (1957) The Student Physician: Introducing Studies in the Sociology of Medical Education, Cambridge, Mass.: Harvard University Press
Miller, C.M.L. and Parlett, M. (1974) Up to the Mark, London: Society for Research into Higher Education
Miller, G.W. (1970) Success, Failure and Wastage in Higher Education, London: Harrap
Mitchell, J. and Oakley, A. (eds.) (1976) The Rights and Wrongs of Women, Harmondsworth: Penguin
Maynard, A. (1975) Experiment with Choice in Education. Hobard Paper 64, London: Institute of Economic Affairs
Moodie, G.C. and Eustace, R. (1974) Power and Authority in British Universities, London: Allen and Unwin
Morris, B.S. (1967) International Community, London N.U.S.
Nuffield Foundation (1974) The Drift of Change. An Interim Report of the Group for Research and Innovation in Higher Education, London: The Nuffield Foundation
Nuffield Foundation (1976) Learning from Learners: A study of the student's experience of academic life. A case study prepared by the Group for Research and Innovation in Higher Education, London: The Nuffield Foundation
Nuffield Foundation (1976) The Container Revolution A critical review of unit and modular degree programmes and their implications for staff and students. Report by the Group for Research and Innovation in Higher Education, London: The Nuffield Foundation
The Observer (1983) Colour Supplement, London: The

References

      Observer, 25th September, 33
Oxtoby, R. (ed.) (1981) Higher Education at the Cross Roads: papers presented at the Sixtieth Annual Conference of the S.R.H.E., 1980, London: Society for Research into Higher Education
Oxtoby, R. (1981) Where do we go from here? In Oxtoby, R. (ed.)
Parlett, M. and Hamilton, D. (1972) Evaluation as Illumination: a new approach to the study of innovatory programmes. Occasional paper 9, Edinburgh: Centre for Research in the Educational Sciences, University of Edinburgh
Percy, K.A. (1983) Review of Wright, J. 1982. In Studies in Higher Education, 8, 1, 95-96
Percy, K.A. and Salter, F.W. (1976) Student and Staff Perceptions and the "Pursuit of Excellence" in British Higher Education. In Higher Education, 5
Psacharopoulos, G. and Layard, R. (1979) Human Capital and Earnings: British Evidence and a Critique. In Review of Economic Studies, 46, 485-503
Raaheim, K. and Wankowski, J. (1981) Helping Students to Learn at University, Bergen: Sigma Forlag
Ramsden, P. (1979) Student learning and perceptions of the academic environment. In Higher Education, 8, 411-427
Ramsden, P. (1981) How Academic Departments Influence Student Learning. In Oxtoby, R. (ed.) 62-68
Robbins' Report (1963) Higher Education. Report of the Committee appointed by the Prime-Minister, under the Chairmanship of Lord Robbins, 1961-63, London: H.M.S.O., Cmnd. 2154
Roe, E. and Biggs, S. (1975) Students, lecturers and librarians: a study of some problems of communication. Report of an investigation carried out by the Tertiary Education Institute, St. Lucia: University of Queensland
Rubenstein, D. and Stoneman, C. (eds.) (1970) Education for Democracy, Harmondsworth: Penguin
Ryle, A. (1969) Student Casualties, London: Allen Lane, The Penguin Press
Schwartz, M.S. and Schwartz, G.G, (1955) Problems in Participant Observation. In American Journal of Sociology, LX, 344
Scrivener, J.E. (1972) Instruction in library use: the persisting problem. In Australian Academic and Research Libraries, 3, 2, 87-118
Sen, A. (1970) Problems of Overseas Students and

References

Nurses, Slough: N.F.E.R.
Shattock, M. and Walker, P. (1977) Factors influencing student choice of university. In Research in Education, 18
Shaw, G.B. (1914) Parents and Children, the Preface to Misalliance, London: Constable, xli
Smithers, A. and Collings, J. (1981) Girls studying Science in the sixth forms. In Kelly, A. (ed.)
Social Trends, No. 12 (1982), London: H.M.S.O., Central Statistics Office
Startup, R. (1979) The University Teacher and his World. Saxon House
The Sunday Times Magazine (1983), London: The Sunday Times, 11th September, 44
Trow, M.A. and Halsey, A.H. (1971) The British Academics, London: Faber and Faber
Truscott, B. (1946) First Year at University, London: Faber and Faber
Turner, R. (ed.) (1974) Ethnomethodology, Harmondsworth: Penguin
University Central Council on Admissions (1982) Nineteenth Report, 1980-81, Cheltenham: UCCA
University of York (1962) Development Plan, 1962-1972, York: University of York
University of York (1982) Admissions' Report, 1981-82, York: University of York
University of York (1983) Undergraduate Prospectus, 1984-85, York: University of York
Wagner, L. (ed.) (1982) Agenda for Institutional Change in Higher Education. Report of a seminar sponsored by the Leverhulme Trust. London: Society for Research into Higher Education
Walton, A. (1982) Private communication based on work in progress investigating the experience of women Science students. London: University of London, Westfield College
Ward, J.P. (1977) Students taking undergraduate courses in Education. In Journal of Further and Higher Education, 1, 1
2.W.L.R. (1983) Regina v. Barnet London Borough Council, Ex Parte Nilish Shah. In The Weekly Law Reports, vol.2, 14th January, 16-34
Weinreich-Haste, H. (1978a) Sex differences in 'fear of success' among British students. In British Journal of Social and Clinical Psychology, 17, 37-43
Weinrich-Haste, H. (1978b) Stereotyping: the sex factor. In Psychology Today, June, 2-25
Weinrich-Haste, H. (1981) The image of science. In Kelly, A. (ed.)
Wieder, D.L. (1974) Telling the Code. In Turner, R.(ed.)

References

Wilby, P. (1976) The New Universities. Series of articles in the Times Higher Educational Supplement, Nos. 225, 227, 229, 231, 236, 238, 239, 241, 243

Wilson, J.D. (1982) Student Learning in Higher Education, London: Croom Helm

Wright, J. (1982) Learning to Learn in Higher Education, London: Croom Helm

Young, M.F.D. (ed.) (1971) Knowledge and Control: New Directions for the Sociology of Education, London: Collier-Macmillan

For Product Safety Concerns and Information please contact our EU representative GPSR@taylorandfrancis.com
Taylor & Francis Verlag GmbH, Kaufingerstraße 24, 80331 München, Germany

www.ingramcontent.com/pod-product-compliance
Lightning Source LLC
Chambersburg PA
CBHW070736230426
43669CB00031B/2452